Detroit Tigers 2021

A Baseball Companion

Edited by Steven Goldman and Bret Sayre

Baseball Prospectus

Craig Brown, Associate Editor
Robert Au, Harry Pavlidis and Amy Pircher, Statistics Editors

Copyright © 2021 by DIY Baseball, LLC.
All rights reserved

This book or any part thereof may not be reproduced or transmitted in any form or by any means, electronic or mechanical, including photocopying, recording, or by any information storage and retrieval system, without permission in writing from the publisher.

Limit of Liability/Disclaimer of Warranty: While the publisher and the author have used their best efforts in preparing this book, they make no representations or warranties with respect to the accuracy or completeness of the contents of this book and specifically disclaim any implied warranties of merchantability or fitness for a particular purpose. No warranty may be created or extended by sales representatives or written sales materials. The advice and strategies contained herein may not be suitable for your situation. You should consult with a professional where appropriate. Neither the publisher nor the author shall be liable for any loss of profit or any other commercial damages, including but not limited to special, incidental, consequential, or other damages.

Library of Congress Cataloging-in-Publication Data:
paperback
ISBN-13: 978-1-950716-43-2

Project Credits
Cover Design: Ginny Searle
Interior Design and Production: Amy Pircher, Robert Au
Layout: Amy Pircher, Robert Au

Baseball icon courtesy of Uberux, from https://www.shareicon.net/author/uberux

Ballpark diagram courtesy of Lou Spirito/THIRTY81 Project, https://thirty81project.com/

Manufactured in the United States of America
10 9 8 7 6 5 4 3 2 1

Table of Contents

Statistical Introduction v

Part 1: Team Analysis
Performance Graphs 3
2020 Team Performance 4
2021 Team Projections 5
Team Personnel 6
Comerica Park Stats 7
Tigers Team Analysis 9

Part 2: Player Analysis
Tigers Player Analysis 14
Tigers Prospects 91

Part 3: Featured Articles
Tigers All-Time Top 10 Players 103
    by Rob Mains

A Taxonomy of 2020 Abnormalities 109
    by Rob Mains

Tranches of WAR 115
    by Russell A. Carleton

Secondhand Sport 121
    by Patrick Dubuque

Steve Dalkowski Dreaming 125
    by Steven Goldman

A Reward For A Functioning Society 129
    by Cory Frontin and Craig Goldstein

Index of Names 133

Statistical Introduction

Sports are, fundamentally, a blend of athletic endeavor and storytelling. Baseball, like any other sport, tells its stories in so many ways: in the arc of a game from the stands or a season from the box scores, in photos, or even in numbers. At Baseball Prospectus, we understand that statistics don't replace observation or any of baseball's stories, but complement everything else that makes the game so much fun.

What stats help us with is with patterns and precision, variance and value. This book can help you learn things you may not see from watching a game or hundred, whether it's the path of a career over time or the breadth of the entire MLB. We'd also never ask you to choose between our numbers and the experience of viewing a game from the cheap seats or the comfort of your home; our publication combines running the numbers with observations and wisdom from some of the brightest minds we can find. But if you *do* want to learn more about the numbers beyond what's on the backs of player jerseys, let us help explain.

Offense

We've revised our methodology for determining batting value. Long-time readers of the book will notice that we've retired True Average in favor of a new metric: Deserved Runs Created Plus (DRC+). Developed by Jonathan Judge and our stats team, this statistic measures everything a player does at the plate–reaching base, hitting for power, making outs, and moving runners over–and puts it on a scale where 100 equals league-average performance. A DRC+ of 150 is terrific, a DRC+ of 100 is average and a DRC+ of 75 means you better be an excellent defender.

DRC+ also does a better job than any of our previous metrics in taking contextual factors into account. The model adjusts for how the park affects performance, but also for things like the talent of the opposing pitcher, value of different types of batted-ball events, league, temperature and other factors. It's able to describe a player's expected offensive contribution than any other statistic we've found over the years, and also does a better job of predicting future performance as well.

The other aspect of run-scoring is baserunning, which we quantify using Baserunning Runs. BRR not only records the value of stolen bases (or getting caught in the act), but also accounts for all the stuff that doesn't show up on the back of a baseball card: a runner's ability to go first to third on a single, or advance on a fly ball.

Defense

Where offensive value is *relatively* easy to identify and understand, defensive value is … not. Over the past dozen years, the sabermetric community has focused mostly on stats based on zone data: a real-live human person records the type of batted ball and estimated landing location, and models are created that give expected outs. From there, you can compare fielders' actual outs to those expected ones. Simple, right?

Unfortunately, zone data has two major issues. First, zone data is recorded by commercial data providers who keep the raw data private unless you pay for it. (All the statistics we build in this book and on our website use public data as inputs.) That hurts our ability to test assumptions or duplicate results. Second, over the years it has become apparent that there's quite a bit of "noise" in zone-based fielding analysis. Sometimes the conclusions drawn from zone data don't hold up to scrutiny, and sometimes the different data provided by different providers don't look anything alike, giving wildly different results. Sometimes the hard-working professional stringers or scorers might unknowingly inflict unconscious bias into the mix: for example good fielders will often be credited with more expected outs despite the data, and ballparks with high press boxes tend to score more line drives than ones with a lower press box.

Enter our Fielding Runs Above Average (FRAA). For most positions, FRAA is built from play-by-play data, which allows us to avoid the subjectivity found in many other fielding metrics. The idea is this: count how many fielding plays are made by a given player and compare that to expected plays for an average fielder at their position (based on pitcher ground ball tendencies and batter handedness). Then we adjust for park and base-out situations.

When it comes to catchers, our methodology is a little different thanks to the laundry list of responsibilities they're tasked with beyond just, well, catching and throwing the ball. By now you've probably heard about "framing" or the art of making umpires more likely to call balls outside the strike zone for strikes. To put this into one tidy number, we incorporate pitch tracking data (for the years it exists) and adjust for important factors like pitcher, umpire, batter and home-field advantage using a mixed-model approach. This grants us a number for how many strikes the catcher is personally adding to (or subtracting from) his pitchers' performance … which we then convert to runs added or lost using linear weights.

Framing is one of the biggest parts of determining catcher value, but we also take into account blocking balls from going past, whether a scorer deems it a passed ball or a wild pitch. We use a similar approach—one that really benefits from the pitch tracking data that tells us what ends up in the dirt and what doesn't. We also include a catcher's ability to prevent stolen bases and how well they field balls in play, and *finally* we come up with our FRAA for catchers.

Pitching

Both pitching and fielding make up the half of baseball that isn't run scoring: run prevention. Separating pitching from fielding is a tough task, and most recent pitching analysis has branched off from Voros McCracken's famous (and controversial) statement, "There is little if any difference among major-league pitchers in their ability to prevent hits on balls hit in the field of play." The research of the analytic community has validated this to some extent, and there are a host of "defense-independent" pitching measures that have been developed to try and extract the effect of the defense behind a hurler from the pitcher's work.

Our solution to this quandary is Deserved Run Average (DRA), our core pitching metric. DRA seeks to evaluate a pitcher's performance, much like earned run average (ERA), the tried-and-true pitching stat you've seen on every baseball broadcast or box score from the past century, but it's very different. To start, DRA takes an event-by-event look at what the pitchers does, and adjusts the value of that event based on different environmental factors like park, batter, catcher, umpire, base-out situation, run differential, inning, defense, home field advantage, pitcher role and temperature. That mixed model gives us a pitcher's expected contribution, similar to what we do for our DRC+ model for hitters and FRAA model for catchers. (Oh, and we also consider the pitcher's effect on basestealing and on balls getting past the catcher.)

DRA is set to the scale of runs allowed per nine innings (RA9) instead of ERA, which makes DRA's scale slightly higher than ERA's. Because of this, for ease of use, we're supplying DRA-, which is much easier for the reader to parse. As with DRC+, DRA- is an "index" stat, meaning instead of using some arbitrary and shifting number to denote what's "good," average is always 100. The reason that it uses a minus rather than a plus is because like ERA, a lower number is better. Therefore a 75 DRA- describes a performance 25 percent better than average, whereas a 150 DRA- means that either a pitcher is getting extremely lucky with their results, or getting ready to try a new pitch.

Since the last time you picked up an edition of this book, we've also made a few minor changes to DRA to make it better. Recent research into "tunneling"—the act of throwing consecutive pitches that appear similar from a batter's point of view until after the swing decision point–data has given us a new contextual factor to account for in DRA: plate distance. This refers to the distance between successive pitches as they approach the plate, and while it has a smaller effect than factors like velocity or whiff rate, it still can help explain pitcher strikeout rate in our model.

Recently Added Descriptive Statistics

Returning to our 2021 edition of the book are a few figures which recently appeared. These numbers may be a little bit more familiar to those of you who have spent some time investigating baseball statistics.

Fastball Percentage

Our fastball percentage (FA%) statistic measures how frequently a pitcher throws a pitch classified as a "fastball," measured as a percentage of overall pitches thrown. We qualify three types of fastballs:

1. The traditional four-seam fastball;
2. The two-seam fastball or sinker;
3. "Hard cutters," which are pitches that have the movement profile of a cut fastball and are used as the pitcher's primary offering or in place of a more traditional fastball.

For example, a pitcher with a FA% of 67 throws any combination of these three pitches about two-thirds of the time.

Whiff Rate

Everybody loves a swing and a miss, and whiff rate (Whiff%) measures how frequently pitchers induce a swinging strike. To calculate Whiff%, we add up all the pitches thrown that ended with a swinging strike, then divide that number by a pitcher's total pitches thrown. Most often, high whiff rates correlate with high strikeout rates (and overall effective pitcher performance).

Called Strike Probability

Called Strike Probability (CSP) is a number that represents the likelihood that all of a pitcher's pitches will be called a strike while controlling for location, pitcher and batter handedness, umpire and count. Here's how it works: on each pitch, our model determines how many times (out of 100) that a similar pitch was called for a strike given those factors mentioned above, and when normalized for each batter's strike zone. Then we average the CSP for all pitches thrown by a pitcher in a season, and that gives us the yearly CSP percentage you see in the stats boxes.

As you might imagine, pitchers with a higher CSP are more likely to work in the zone, where pitchers with a lower CSP are likely locating their pitches outside the normal strike zone, for better or for worse.

Projections

Many of you aren't turning to this book just for a look at what a player has done, but for a look at what a player is going to do: the PECOTA projections. PECOTA, initially developed by Nate Silver (who has moved on to greater fame as a political analyst), consists of three parts:

1. Major-league equivalencies, which use minor-league statistics to project how a player will perform in the major leagues;
2. Baseline forecasts, which use weighted averages and regression to the mean to estimate a player's current true talent level; and
3. Aging curves, which uses the career paths of comparable players to estimate how a player's statistics are likely to change over time.

With all those important things covered, let's take a look at what's in the book this year.

Team Prospectus

Most of this book is composed of team chapters, with one for each of the 30 major-league franchises. On the first page of each chapter, you'll see a box that contains some of the key statistics for each team as well as a very inviting stadium diagram.

We start with the team name, their unadjusted 2020 win-loss record, and their divisional ranking. Beneath that are a host of other team statistics. **Pythag** presents an adjusted 2020 winning percentage, calculated by taking runs scored per game (**RS/G**) and runs allowed per game (**RA/G**) for the team, and running them through a version of Bill James' Pythagorean formula that was refined and improved by David Smyth and Brandon Heipp. (The formula is called "Pythagenpat," which is equally fun to type and to say.)

Next up is **DRC+**, described earlier, to indicate the overall hitting ability of the team either above or below league-average. Run prevention on the pitching side is covered by **DRA** (also mentioned earlier) and another metric: Fielding Independent Pitching (**FIP**), which calculates another ERA-like statistic based on strikeouts, walks, and home runs recorded. Defensive Efficiency Rating (**DER**) tells us the percentage of balls in play turned into outs for the team, and is a quick fielding shorthand that rounds out run prevention.

After that, we have several measures related to roster composition, as opposed to on-field performance. **B-Age** and **P-Age** tell us the average age of a team's batters and pitchers, respectively. **Payroll** is the combined team payroll for all on-field players, and Doug Pappas' Marginal Dollars per Marginal Win (**M$/MW**) tells us how much money a team spent to earn production above replacement level.

Next to each of these stats, we've listed each team's MLB rank in that category from first to 30th. In this, first always indicates a positive outcome and 30th a negative outcome, except in the case of salary—first is highest.

After the franchise statistics, we share a few items about the team's home ballpark. There's the aforementioned diagram of the park's dimensions (including distances to the outfield wall), a graphic showing the height of the wall from the left-field pole to the right-field pole, and a table showing three-year park factors for the stadium. The park factors are displayed as indexes where 100 is average, 110 means that the park inflates the statistic in question by 10 percent, and 90 means that the park deflates the statistic in question by 10 percent.

On the second page of each team chapter, you'll find three graphs. The first is **Payroll History** and helps you see how the team's payroll has compared to the MLB and divisional average payrolls over time. Payroll figures are current as of January 1, 2021; with so many free agents still unsigned as of this writing, the final 2021 figure will likely be significantly different for many teams. (In the meantime, you can always find the most current data at Baseball Prospectus' Cot's Baseball Contracts page.)

The second graph is **Future Commitments** and helps you see the team's future outlays, if any.

The third graph is **Farm System Ranking** and displays how the Baseball Prospectus prospect team has ranked the organization's farm system since 2007.

After the graphs, we have a **Personnel** section that lists many of the important decision-makers and upper-level field and operations staff members for the franchise, as well as any former Baseball Prospectus staff members who are currently part of the organization. (In very rare circumstances, someone might be on both lists!)

Position Players

After all that information and a thoughtful bylined essay covering each team, we present our player comments. These are also bylined, but due to frequent franchise shifts during the offseason, our bylines are more a rough guide than a perfect accounting of who wrote what.

Each player is listed with the major-league team that employed him as of early January 2021. If a player changed teams after that point via free agency, trade, or any other method, you'll be able to find them in the chapter for their previous squad.

As an example, take a look at the player comment for Padres shortstop Fernando Tatis Jr.: the stat block that accompanies his written comment is at the top of this page. First we cover biographical information (age is as of June 30, 2021) before moving onto the stats themselves. Our statistic columns include standard identifying information like **YEAR**, **TEAM**, **LVL** (level of affiliated play) and **AGE** before getting into the numbers. Next, we provide raw, untranslated

Fernando Tatis Jr. SS
Born: 01/02/99 Age: 22 Bats: R Throws: R
Height: 6'3" Weight: 217 Origin: International Free Agent, 2015

YEAR	TEAM	LVL	AGE	PA	R	2B	3B	HR	RBI	BB	K	SB	CS	AVG/OBP/SLG
2018	SA	AA	19	394	77	22	4	16	43	33	109	16	5	.286/.355/.507
2019	SD	MLB	20	372	61	13	6	22	53	30	110	16	6	.317/.379/.590
2020	SD	MLB	21	257	50	11	2	17	45	27	61	11	3	.277/.366/.571
2021 FS	SD	MLB	22	600	95	24	4	31	81	50	165	17	8	.263/.331/.499
2021 DC	SD	MLB	22	628	100	25	4	32	85	53	173	19	8	.263/.331/.499

Comparables: Darryl Strawberry, Bo Bichette, Ronald Acuña Jr.

YEAR	TEAM	LVL	AGE	PA	DRC+	BABIP	BRR	FRAA	WARP
2018	SA	AA	19	394	136	.370	3.0	SS(83): -1.9	2.4
2019	SD	MLB	20	372	118	.410	7.1	SS(83): 0.9	3.4
2020	SD	MLB	21	257	126	.306	0.7	SS(57): -5.5	0.9
2021 FS	SD	MLB	22	600	126	.318	1.7	SS -1	3.9
2021 DC	SD	MLB	22	628	126	.318	1.8	SS -1	4.0

numbers like you might find on the back of your dad's baseball cards: **PA** (plate appearances), **R** (runs), **2B** (doubles), **3B** (triples), **HR** (home runs), **RBI** (runs batted in), **BB** (walks), **K** (strikeouts), **SB** (stolen bases) and **CS** (caught stealing).

Following the basic stats is **Whiff%** (whiff rate), which denotes how often, when a batter swings, he fails to make contact with the ball. Another way to think of this number is an inverse of a hitter's contact rate.

Next, we have unadjusted "slash" statistics: **AVG** (batting average), **OBP** (on-base percentage) and **SLG** (slugging percentage). Following the slash line is **DRC+** (Deserved Runs Created Plus), which we described earlier as total offensive expected contribution compared to the league average.

BABIP (batting average on balls in play) tells us how often a ball in play fell for a hit, and can help us identify whether a batter may have been lucky or not ... but note that high BABIPs also tend to follow the great hitters of our time, as well as speedy singles hitters who put the ball on the ground.

The next item is **BRR** (Baserunning Runs), which covers all of a player's baserunning accomplishments including (but not limited to) swiped bags and failed attempts. Next is **FRAA** (Fielding Runs Above Average), which also includes the number of games previously played at each position noted in parentheses. Multi-position players have only their two most frequent positions listed here, but their total FRAA number reflects all positions played.

Our last column here is **WARP** (Wins Above Replacement Player). WARP estimates the total value of a player, which means for hitters it takes into account hitting runs above average (calculated using the DRC+ model), BRR and FRAA. Then, it makes an adjustment for positions played and gives the player a credit for plate appearances based upon the difference between "replacement level"—which is derived from the quality of players added to a team's roster after the start of the season–and the league average.

The final line just below the stats box is **PECOTA** data, which is discussed further in a following section.

Catchers

Catchers are a special breed, and thus they have earned their own separate box which displays some of the defensive metrics that we've built just for them. As an example, let's check out Yasmani Grandal.

YEAR	TEAM	P. COUNT	FRM RUNS	BLK RUNS	THRW RUNS	TOT RUNS
2018	LAD	16816	15.7	0.8	0.1	16.5
2019	MIL	18740	19.4	1.8	-0.1	21.1
2020	CHW	4830	3.7	0.3	-0.2	3.8
2021	CHW	14430	16.7	-0.6	1.0	17.1
2021	CHW	14430	16.7	0.4	1.0	18.0

The **YEAR** and **TEAM** columns match what you'd find in the other stat box. **P. COUNT** indicates the number of pitches thrown while the catcher was behind the plate, including swinging strikes, fouls and balls in play. **FRM RUNS** is the total run value the catcher provided (or cost) his team by influencing the umpire to call strikes where other catchers did not. **BLK RUNS** expresses the total run value above or below average for the catcher's ability to prevent wild pitches and passed balls. **THRW RUNS** is calculated using a similar model as the previous two statistics, and it measures a catcher's ability to throw out basestealers but also to dissuade them from testing his arm in the first place. It takes into account factors like the pitcher (including his delivery and pickoff move) and baserunner (who could be as fast as Billy Hamilton or as slow as Yonder Alonso). **TOT RUNS** is the sum of all of the previous three statistics.

Pitchers

Let's give our pitchers a turn, using 2020 AL Cy Young winner Shane Bieber as our example. Take a look at his stat block: the first line and the **YEAR**, **TEAM**, **LVL** and **AGE** columns are the same as in the position player example earlier.

Here too, we have a series of columns that display raw, unadjusted statistics compiled by the pitcher over the course of a season: **W** (wins), **L** (losses), **SV** (saves), **G** (games pitched), **GS** (games started), **IP** (innings pitched), **H** (hits allowed) and **HR** (home runs allowed). Next we have two statistics that are rates: **BB/9** (walks per nine innings) and **K/9** (strikeouts per nine innings), before returning to the unadjusted K (strikeouts).

Next up is **GB%** (ground ball percentage), which is the percentage of all batted balls that were hit on the ground, including both outs and hits. Remember, this is based on observational data and subject to human error, so please approach this with a healthy dose of skepticism.

BABIP (batting average on balls in play) is calculated using the same methodology as it is for position players, but it often tells us more about a pitcher than it does a hitter. With pitchers, a high BABIP is often due to poor defense or bad luck, and can often be an indicator of potential rebound, and a low BABIP may be cause to expect performance regression. (A typical league-average BABIP is close to .290-.300.)

The metrics **WHIP** (walks plus hits per inning pitched) and **ERA** (earned run average) are old standbys: WHIP measures walks and hits allowed on a per-inning basis, while ERA measures earned runs on a nine-inning basis. Neither of these stats are translated or adjusted.

DRA- (Deserved Run Average) was described at length earlier, and measures how the pitcher "deserved" to perform compared to other pitchers. Please note that since we lack all the data points that would make for a "real" DRA for minor-league events, the DRA- displayed for minor league partial-seasons is based off of different data. (That data is a modified version of our cFIP metric, which you can find more information about on our website.)

Shane Bieber   RHP

Born: 05/31/95   Age: 26   Bats: R   Throws: R
Height: 6'3"   Weight: 200   Origin: Round 4, 2016 Draft (#122 overall)

YEAR	TEAM	LVL	AGE	W	L	SV	G	GS	IP	H	HR	BB/9	K/9	K	GB%	BABIP
2018	AKR	AA	23	3	0	0	5	5	31	26	1	0.3	8.7	30	47.3%	.278
2018	COL	AAA	23	3	1	0	8	8	48^2	30	3	1.1	8.7	47	52.0%	.227
2018	CLE	MLB	23	11	5	0	20	19	114^2	130	13	1.8	9.3	118	46.2%	.356
2019	CLE	MLB	24	15	8	0	34	33	214^1	186	31	1.7	10.9	259	44.4%	.298
2020	CLE	MLB	25	8	1	0	12	12	77^1	46	7	2.4	14.2	122	48.4%	.267
2021 FS	CLE	MLB	26	10	6	0	26	26	150	121	18	2.1	11.7	195	45.5%	.297
2021 DC	CLE	MLB	26	14	7	0	30	30	196.7	159	24	2.1	11.7	257	45.5%	.297

Comparables: Luis Severino, Danny Salazar, Joe Musgrove

YEAR	TEAM	LVL	AGE	WHIP	ERA	DRA-	WARP	MPH	FB%	WHF	CSP
2018	AKR	AA	23	0.87	1.16	61	0.9				
2018	COL	AAA	23	0.74	1.66	69	1.2				
2018	CLE	MLB	23	1.33	4.55	74	2.6	94.7	57.4%	26.2%	
2019	CLE	MLB	24	1.05	3.28	75	4.9	94.4	45.8%	30.8%	
2020	CLE	MLB	25	0.87	1.63	53	2.6	95.3	53.6%	40.7%	
2021 FS	CLE	MLB	26	1.04	2.44	64	4.4	94.7	50.0%	33.2%	44.2%
2021 DC	CLE	MLB	26	1.04	2.44	64	5.8	94.7	50.0%	33.2%	44.2%

Just like with hitters, **WARP** (Wins Above Replacement Player) is a total value metric that puts pitchers of all stripes on the same scale as position players. We use DRA as the primary input for our calculation of WARP. You might notice that relief pitchers (due to their limited innings) may have a lower WARP than you were expecting or than you might see in other WARP-like metrics. WARP does not take leverage into account, just the actions a pitcher performs and the expected value of those actions ... which ends up judging high-leverage relief pitchers differently than you might imagine given their prestige and market value.

MPH gives you the pitcher's 95th percentile velocity for the noted season, in order to give you an idea of what the *peak* fastball velocity a pitcher possesses. Since this comes from our pitch-tracking data, it is not publicly available for minor-league pitchers.

Finally, we display the three new pitching metrics we described earlier. **FB%** (fastball percentage) gives you the percentage of fastballs thrown out of all pitches. **WHF** (whiff rate) tells you the percentage of swinging strikes induced out of all pitches. **CSP** (called strike probability) expresses the likelihood of all pitches thrown to result in a called strike, after controlling for factors like handedness, umpire, pitch type, count and location.

PECOTA

All players have PECOTA projections for 2021, as well as a set of other numbers that describe the performance of comparable players according to PECOTA. All projections for 2021 are for the player at the date we went to press in early January and are projected into the league and park context as indicated by the team abbreviation. (Note that players at very low levels of the minors are too unpredictable to assess using these numbers.) All PECOTA projected statistics represent a player's projected major-league performance.

How we're doing that is a little different this season. There are really two different values that go into the final stat line that you see for PECOTA: How a player performs, and how much playing time he'll be given to perform it. In the past we've estimated playing time based on each team's roster and depth charts, and we'll continue to do that. These projections are denoted as **2021 DC**.

But in many cases, a player won't be projected for major-league playing time; most of the time this is because they aren't projected to be major-league players at all, but still developing as prospects. Or perhaps a player will provide Triple-A depth, only to have an opportunity open up because of injury. For these purposes, we're also supplying a second projection, labeled **2021 FS**, or full season. This is what we would project the player to provide in 600 plate appearances or 150 innings pitched.

Below the projections are the player's three highest-scoring comparable players as determined by PECOTA. All comparables represent a snapshot of how the listed player was performing at the same age as the current player, so if a

23-year-old pitcher is compared to Bartolo Colón, he's actually being compared to a 23-year-old Colón, not the version that pitched for the Rangers in 2018, nor to Colón's career as a whole.

A few points about pitcher projections. First, we aren't yet projecting peak velocity, so that column will be blank in the PECOTA lines. Second, projecting DRA is trickier than evaluating past performance, because it is unclear how deserving each pitcher will be of his anticipated outcomes. However, we know that another DRA-related statistic–contextual FIP or cFIP-estimates future run scoring very well. So for PECOTA, the projected DRA- figures you see are based on the past cFIPs generated by the pitcher and comparable players over time, along with the other factors described above.

If you're familiar with PECOTA, then you'll have noticed that the projection system often appears bullish on players coming off a bad year and bearish on players coming off a good year. (This is because the system weights several previous seasons, not just the most recent one.) In addition, we publish the 50th percentile projections for each player–which is smack in the middle of the range of projected production—which tends to mean PECOTA stat lines don't often have extreme results like 40 home runs or 250 strikeouts in a given season. In essence, PECOTA doesn't project very many extreme seasons.

Managers

After all those wonderful team chapters, we've got statistics for each big-league manager, all of whom are organized by alphabetical order. Here you'll find a block including an extraordinary amount of information collected from each manager's entire career. For more information on the acronyms and what they mean, please visit the Glossary at www.baseballprospectus.com.

There is one important metric that we'd like to call attention to, and you'll find it next to each manager's name: **wRM+** (weighted reliever management plus). Developed by Rob Arthur and Rian Watt, wRM+ investigates how good a manager is at using their best relievers during the moments of highest leverage, using both our proprietary DRA metric as well as Leverage Index. wRM+ is scaled to a league average of 100, and a wRM+ of 105 indicates that relievers were used approximately five percent "better" than average. On the other hand, a wRM+ of 95 would tell us the team used its relievers five percent "worse" than the average team.

While wRM+ does not have an extremely strong correlation with a manager, it is statistically significant; this means that a manager is not *entirely* responsible for a team's wRM+, but does have some effect on that number.

Part 1: Team Analysis

Performance Graphs

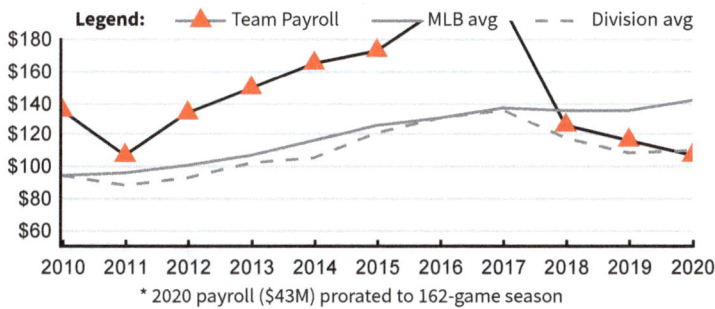

Payroll History (in millions)

* 2020 payroll ($43M) prorated to 162-game season

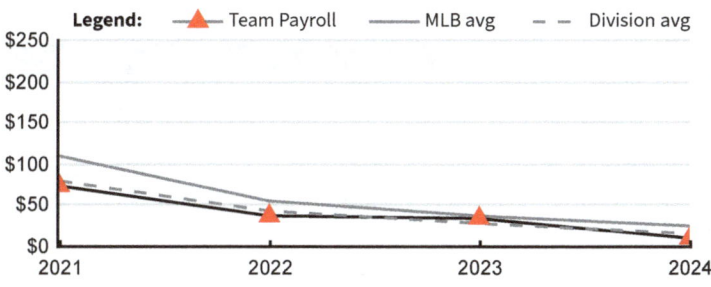

Future Commitments (in millions)

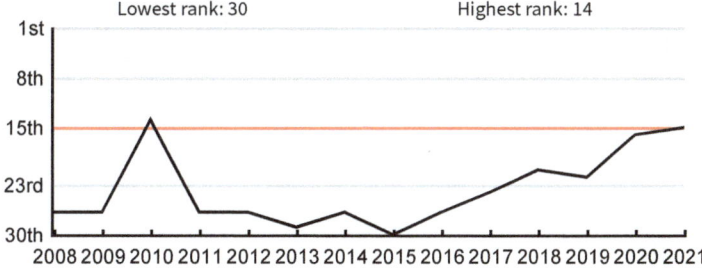

Farm System Ranking

Lowest rank: 30   Highest rank: 14

2020 Team Performance

ACTUAL STANDINGS

Team	W	L	Pct
MIN	36	24	0.600
CHW	35	25	0.583
CLE	35	25	0.583
KC	26	34	0.433
DET	**23**	**35**	**0.397**

dWIN% STANDINGS

Team	W	L	Pct
CLE	30	30	0.506
MIN	29	31	0.498
CHW	27	33	0.456
KC	24	36	0.403
DET	**19**	**41**	**0.333**

TOP HITTERS

Player	WARP
Jeimer Candelario	1.0
Jonathan Schoop	0.6
Victor Reyes	0.5

TOP PITCHERS

Player	WARP
Spencer Turnbull	0.9
Daniel Norris	0.6
José Cisnero	0.5

VITAL STATISTICS

Statistic Name	Value	Rank
Pythagenpat	.384	27th
dWin%	.333	29th
Runs Scored per Game	4.29	22nd
Runs Allowed per Game	5.48	28th
Deserved Runs Created Plus	88	28th
Deserved Run Average Minus	119	29th
Fielding Independent Pitching	5.21	29th
Defensive Efficiency Rating	.693	20th
Batter Age	28.1	14th
Pitcher Age	27.1	5th
Payroll	$43.0M	22nd
Marginal $ per Marginal Win	$4.5M	19th

2021 Team Projections

PROJECTED STANDINGS

Team	W	L	Pct	+/-
MIN	90.8	71.2	0.560	-6
With Nelson Cruz returning and Andrelton Simmons, J.A. Happ, and Alex Colomé on board the Twins seem like a balanced behemoth again.				
CLE	85.0	77.0	0.525	-9
That they've lost so many great players is an indictment of ownership. That they remain respectable is a testament to the agility of the front office.				
CHW	82.8	79.2	0.511	-11
Lance Lynn and Liam Hendriks give Tony La Russa the paint-by-numbers pitching staff he prefers, and all of the crucial cogs in last year's young lineup return.				
KC	71.5	90.5	0.441	1
Creeping back toward respectability, the Royals added reliable veterans coming off down years and will hope their youth movement gains momentum quickly.				
DET	65.7	96.3	0.406	3
The trend arrow is finally pointing up, but Robbie Grossman and Wilson Ramos qualifying as significant improvements shows they still have a long way to go.				

TOP PROJECTED HITTERS

Player	WARP
Robbie Grossman	1.5
Jonathan Schoop	1.2
Jeimer Candelario	1.0

TOP PROJECTED PITCHERS

Player	WARP
Matthew Boyd	2.1
Spencer Turnbull	1.3
Tarik Skubal	1.1

FARM SYSTEM REPORT

Top Prospect	Number of Top 101 Prospects
Spencer Torkelson, #13	5

KEY DEDUCTIONS

Player	WARP
C.J. Cron	1.3

KEY ADDITIONS

Player	WARP
Robbie Grossman	1.5
Wilson Ramos	0.5
José Ureña	0.5
Nomar Mazara	0.3

Team Personnel

Executive Vice President of Baseball Operations and General Manager
Al Avila

Vice President, Assistant General Manager
David Chadd

Vice President, Player Personnel
Scott Bream

Vice President, Player Development
Dave Littlefield

Manager
A.J. Hinch

Comerica Park Stats

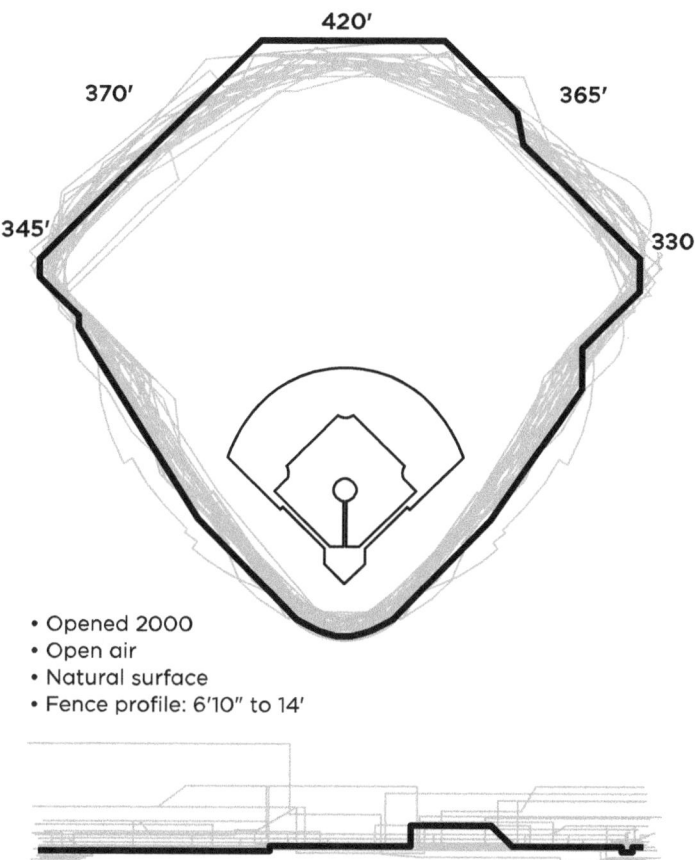

- Opened 2000
- Open air
- Natural surface
- Fence profile: 6'10" to 14'

Three-Year Park Factors

Runs	Runs/RH	Runs/LH	HR/RH	HR/LH
102	104	99	102	97

Tigers Team Analysis

There's a trope that exists in fiction in which a once successful and respected figure, having fallen on hard times or having suffered disgrace, is forced to take on a job of last resort.

Maybe they're a military figure who, after suffering ignominious defeat, has been exiled to a remote, backwater post. Maybe they're a hot-shot politician or businessman who got caught up in scandal and now find themselves as a fish-out-of-water, volunteering for some lost cause or opening up a small shop in a small town. Maybe they're an entertainer who squandered opportunities or committed acts of self-sabotage and find themselves doing dinner theater or pitching reverse mortgages on cable TV. It can be anything, really.

The idea, though, is not that the station they've been reduced to in life is the end point of their character arc. Rather, it's the starting point. The starting point for their redemption quest.

The redemption quest begins with our character in a bad place but one in which they are granted a final chance to do better. Usually, that chance involves a seemingly impossible task. Usually it involves rallying a ragtag band of misfits to do something great. Something no one believed they ever had in them. To take down a formidable enemy. To put on a show. To win the big game. Whatever it is, getting there won't be easy, but our disgraced hero—after experiencing some early bumps in the road—finds a way to transform the ragtag band of misfits from a dysfunctional group of losers into a well-oiled machine. This may or may not involve a training montage. In the end, though, the misfits stand victorious and our disgraced hero stands redeemed.

This, of course, is where A.J. Hinch and the 2021 Detroit Tigers find themselves. They're the Bad News Bears the day Morris Buttermaker shows up, except instead of being a washed up alcoholic, Hinch was a manager who failed to manage his players in a responsible way. They're the Mighty Ducks right after Gordon Bombay is placed in charge of them except, instead of a DUI, Hinch was asleep at the wheel during baseball's biggest cheating scandal in a century. If not for that he'd still be in Houston. If not for the Tigers' run of ineptitude, the gig wouldn't have come available. It's all the more appropriate—and cinematic—that, like so many disgraced heroes in fiction, Hinch's rock bottom features him going home again and starting over, as it were. No, that one season he played for the Tigers in 2003 is not quite as resonant as Gordon Bombay going back to the same peewee hockey league where he starred as a kid, but it's close enough as far as life imitating art goes.

The bunch that is likely to take the field for the 2021 Detroit Tigers is definitely ragtag. And many of them match up to stock characters in the Hollywood versions of this story.

Shortstop Willi Castro and third baseman Jeimer Candelario are what pass for the talented guys who could actually be someplace better but aren't due to circumstance. Hinch will have to teach them how to be engaged in the present rather than looking to the future and teach them how to be leaders. Matthew Boyd, Spencer Turnbull and Michael Fulmer—the embodiment of what has made these sacks so sad over the past few years—will have to be taught to find something more inside of themselves than they thought was there. Youngsters Casey Mize, Tarik Skubal, Spencer Torkelson, Isaac Paredes and Daz Cameron are the green ones who've been brought into a losing culture and need to be shown a different way lest any of that old stuff stick to them in their formative stage. Miguel Cabrera is the past-his-prime graybeard Hinch will ask to give his all and hope for a miracle. Add in some hired guns to work behind the plate and to cover the gaps before the kids establish themselves, and you have a nearly straight-from-central-casting assemblage of misfits.

One can imagine a scenario in which Hinch takes these players—and whatever other players the Tigers acquire over the course of the next couple of years—and molds them into winners. That they take a big step forward, out of the cellar, in 2021 not unlike how the White Sox and the Padres did in 2020. That, in due time, the Tigers are not only good, but are approaching great, and even surpass the level those Justin Verlander and Cabrera-led teams of the Jim Leyland years achieved and win a World Series. If and when that happens, Hinch's redemption quest will be considered complete by most observers. The former champion, knocked off his pedestal and having hit rock bottom, will have completed his climb back to the top. And then the credits will roll.

There's only one problem with that. Setting aside the fact that Hinch is a real person and not a fictional character, his mere athletic success—be it in reality or in fiction—would not be indicia of actual redemption. Of moral redemption. And it is moral redemption Hinch's story requires here, because his failures were moral failures, not athletic ones. A proper story of moral redemption requires that those be addressed and learned from. It requires so much more.

The first thing any student of fiction learns about a moral redemption story is that it requires some shock or disruption in the hero's life. The thing that sends him into a crisis from which he must be redeemed. We'll give Hinch that. He was disgraced with the Astros, got fired and suspended, and now he's managing a last place Tigers team. It's a good start.

The next thing required of a redemption story is the requirement of a seemingly impossible challenge. Given where the Tigers have been for the past few years and where they look to be now, I'd say that beating out the White Sox, Twins and Cleveland as currently constructed qualifies as a challenge. If Hinch plays out the arc as described above, again, he's done it. Two-for-two. Not bad! But now it gets tougher.

In any proper redemption story the hero must, from his low point, and in the face of the big challenge, either discover or rediscover his inner moral code or choose to face it employing his past immoral or amoral path. That's the big turning point, really. Because it's important to note here that Hinch could very well win a World Series with the Tigers having learned nothing from the ignominy he earned in Houston. He could simply do what he always did, benefit from an infusion of talent, and come out on top in the end. If that happens—if Hinch is hoisted upon the shoulders of his players after the final out of a World Series—has he simply found success or has he truly been redeemed?

I figure not many people care about any of those things. In sports, we tend to consider redemption in only the most shallow of ways. We see Michael Vick come back and run for some touchdowns and somehow claim that means something. We see Tiger Woods win a major in his 40s and see it as an appropriate final scene in his redemption story as well. No matter what the scandal or failing of a given sports figure faces or experiences, we're quick to brush aside once they show that they're still able to bring it once the whistle blows or the umpire yells "play ball!" At the same time, if the scandal-bound sports figure does not come back on the field or perform to his old standards, we assume he is not redeemed no matter how deep and healing his actual redemption quest happened to be.

Tigers fans, for sure, aren't going to examine A.J. Hinch's character arc to determine whether his rallying of the ragtag band of misfits satisfied all of the conditions of a proper moral redemption story. To most of them the results will be all that matters. Which, it should be pointed out, is the ethos that got Hinch and the Astros in trouble in the first place. There will be many, however, particularly in the media, who will judge Hinch's redemption arc on a 1-to-1 basis with his won-loss record in Detroit. Who will be the first to consider the success of Willi Castro, Jeimer Candelario, Matthew Boyd, Spencer Turnbull, Michael Fulmer, Casey Mize, Tarik Skubal, Spencer Torkelson, Isaac Paredes, Daz Cameron and, yes, even Miguel Cabrera, to be a direct comment on what lessons Hinch did or did not learn during his year in the wilderness following his dismissal and suspension.

I'd like to think, though, that he'd be held to at least a slightly higher standard. I'd hope that, like Gordon Bombay, Morris Buttermaker and all of the other fallen characters put on the path to redemption, Hinch will learn things about himself and teach things to others while on that path. Things that he would not have known had it not been for his earlier downfall. Things that might make that redemption complete and fulfilling as opposed to the superficial redemption we tend to ascribe to anyone who finds mere success after failure.

I'd like that. I'd like to believe something satisfying like that would happen. But being realistic, I know that's not in the cards. At the very least it's not anything outsiders will ever see, because life isn't the movies, A.J. Hinch isn't a character, real people's lives tend not to follow neat narratives, and redemption is hardly ever a truly public process.

Hinch may learn lessons from his mistakes in Houston. He may become a better person because of those lessons. He may, however, lose 102 games a year with the Tigers before being fired and never give the public any sign that he's grown since January 2020. In contrast he may, notwithstanding his relatively contrite and reflective words since the Astros fired him, learn nothing much at all from his experience apart from the importance of not getting caught doing something wrong, and win 102 games a year and three pennants, all while giving lip service to the sign stealing scandal being a blessing in disguise or a turning point or some such.

No matter what the outcome—one of those two extremes or something in between—we'll never truly know what's in his heart. We're not going to be privy to his actual growth or lack thereof, even if he says so or if the press ascribes those things to him. Unlike the movies, sports do not provide us with that kind of clear view into a character's heart. In light of that, perhaps we shouldn't try to make narratives out of sports figures. A.J. Hinch included.

—*Craig Calcaterra is the writer and editor of the Cup Of Coffee newsletter.*

Part 2: Player Analysis

Detroit Tigers 2021

PLAYER COMMENTS WITH GRAPHS

Jorge Bonifacio   OF
Born: 06/04/93   Age: 28   Bats: R   Throws: R
Height: 6'1"   Weight: 220   Origin: International Free Agent, 2009

YEAR	TEAM	LVL	AGE	PA	R	2B	3B	HR	RBI	BB	K	SB	CS	AVG/OBP/SLG
2018	OMA	AAA	25	58	11	5	1	0	9	7	12	0	0	.392/.466/.529
2018	KC	MLB	25	270	31	16	2	4	23	29	71	0	1	.225/.312/.360
2019	OMA	AAA	26	500	67	18	5	20	62	38	121	6	4	.222/.284/.417
2019	KC	MLB	26	21	3	3	0	0	3	1	7	0	0	.350/.381/.500
2020	DET	MLB	27	94	8	3	0	2	17	5	26	0	0	.221/.277/.326
2021 FS	DET	MLB	28	600	60	23	4	16	65	49	177	0	1	.224/.296/.378

Comparables: Kevin Roberson, Dustan Mohr, Brian Buchanan

Remember the golden age of clutch hitting, which started around when baseball was invented and ended around the mid-2000s? Bonifacio had a season for that age: a 1.301 OPS with runners in scoring position, and .337 otherwise. Data has shown this isn't a projectable skill unless he starts believing in ghosts and then pictures them on base. The one-time Top 101 prospect has struggled to manifest his raw power into actual power and demonstrates the vestiges of athleticism in right field, but has yet to find the one ballpark that is truly haunted. We're not telling you which one it is, either.

YEAR	TEAM	LVL	AGE	PA	DRC+	BABIP	BRR	FRAA	WARP
2018	OMA	AAA	25	58	157	.513	-0.2	RF(13): -1.2	0.3
2018	KC	MLB	25	270	84	.301	0.0	RF(55): -0.8, LF(7): -1.0	-0.1
2019	OMA	AAA	26	500	73	.252	0.4	LF(56): 9.6, RF(42): 3.7	0.8
2019	KC	MLB	26	21	67	.538	-0.3	RF(4): -0.3, LF(1): 0.0	-0.1
2020	DET	MLB	27	94	76	.288	0.3	LF(19): 0.9, RF(10): 0.2	0.0
2021 FS	DET	MLB	28	600	85	.300	-0.3	RF 1, LF 1	0.5

Jorge Bonifacio, continued

Batted Ball Distribution

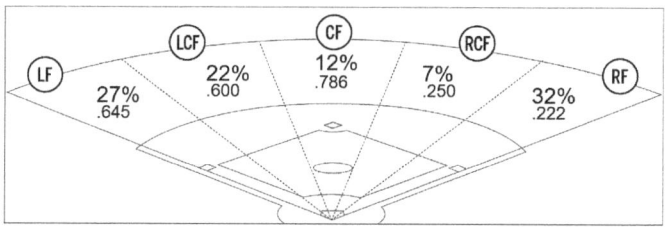

Strike Zone vs LHP   Strike Zone vs RHP

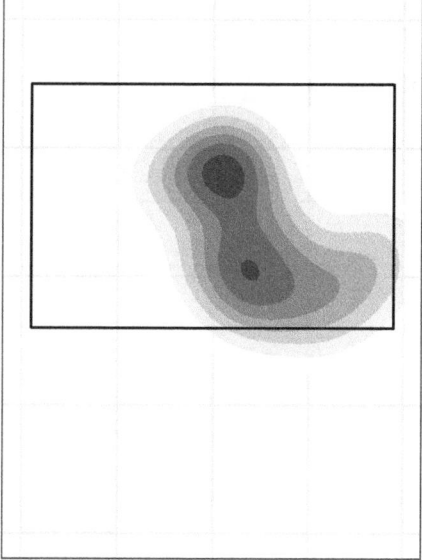

Detroit Tigers 2021

Miguel Cabrera 1B
Born: 04/18/83   Age: 38   Bats: R   Throws: R
Height: 6'4"   Weight: 249   Origin: International Free Agent, 1999

YEAR	TEAM	LVL	AGE	PA	R	2B	3B	HR	RBI	BB	K	SB	CS	AVG/OBP/SLG
2018	DET	MLB	35	157	17	11	0	3	22	22	27	0	0	.299/.395/.448
2019	DET	MLB	36	549	41	21	0	12	59	48	108	0	0	.282/.346/.398
2020	DET	MLB	37	231	28	4	0	10	35	24	51	1	0	.250/.329/.417
2021 FS	DET	MLB	38	600	70	22	1	16	66	65	139	0	1	.242/.329/.382
2021 DC	DET	MLB	38	586	68	21	1	16	65	64	136	0	1	.242/.329/.382

Comparables: Fred McGriff, Lance Berkman, Jason Giambi

No one would have faulted him for climbing stiffly onto that retirement pony and riding it into the sunset, or even getting a fresh start with a playoff team by taking the Verlander's way out. But Cabrera seemed content with cementing his status as the lone recognizable face in an abysmal rebuild. He's holding his own as well, passing icon after icon on the leaderboard while adjusting to hit for power with whatever joints in his limbs still rotate. He ought to pass Ruth in hits, Gehrig in home runs, Ortiz in RBI and possibly Bonds in doubles. In all, a fine season will make him the seventh card-carrying member of the Society of 3,000-500 Gentlemen.

YEAR	TEAM	LVL	AGE	PA	DRC+	BABIP	BRR	FRAA	WARP
2018	DET	MLB	35	157	108	.352	0.5	1B(32): -0.0	0.4
2019	DET	MLB	36	549	100	.336	-4.4	1B(26): -1.5	0.3
2020	DET	MLB	37	231	102	.283	-0.5		0.5
2021 FS	DET	MLB	38	600	99	.297	-0.9	1B 0	0.7
2021 DC	DET	MLB	38	586	99	.297	-0.9		0.8

Miguel Cabrera, continued

Batted Ball Distribution

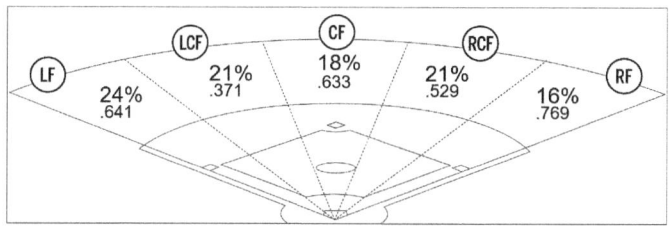

Strike Zone vs LHP   Strike Zone vs RHP

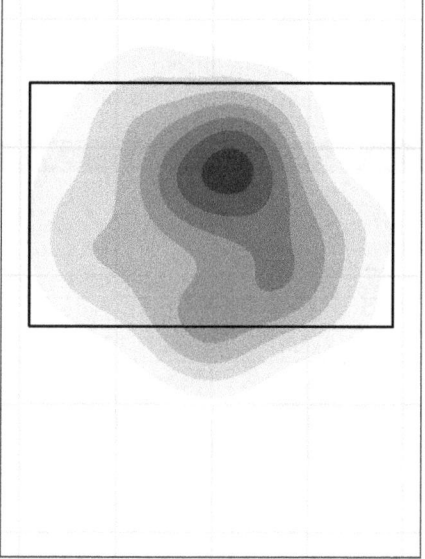

Detroit Tigers 2021

Jeimer Candelario 3B
Born: 11/24/93 Age: 27 Bats: S Throws: R
Height: 6'1" Weight: 221 Origin: International Free Agent, 2010

YEAR	TEAM	LVL	AGE	PA	R	2B	3B	HR	RBI	BB	K	SB	CS	AVG/OBP/SLG
2018	DET	MLB	24	619	78	28	3	19	54	66	160	3	2	.224/.317/.393
2019	TOL	AAA	25	178	30	10	2	9	33	22	35	0	0	.320/.416/.588
2019	DET	MLB	25	386	33	17	2	8	32	43	99	3	1	.203/.306/.337
2020	DET	MLB	26	206	30	11	3	7	29	20	49	1	1	.297/.369/.503
2021 FS	DET	MLB	27	600	68	26	4	17	67	64	153	1	1	.233/.324/.403
2021 DC	DET	MLB	27	571	65	25	4	16	63	61	145	1	1	.233/.324/.403

Comparables: Phil Nevin, Russ Davis, Wilson Betemit

Candelario may be the dramatic type. Not the sports talk radio controversy type, or the Shakespeare in the Park type, but the erratic production from season to season type. It's the worst category of drama for someone trying to stay in the lineup, but after a forgettable 2019 that resulted in a Triple-A demotion, Candelario roared back with conviction, slapping the label off the ball, improving his batting and slugging averages against both fastballs and offspeed pitches equally. His line drive attitude will keep his homer total in the low 20s at best, and his move to first base was more out of roster-based necessity than defensive inferiority. PECOTA doesn't project levels of drama for the 2021 season, but it's unofficially in the "TNT Original Series" range.

YEAR	TEAM	LVL	AGE	PA	DRC+	BABIP	BRR	FRAA	WARP
2018	DET	MLB	24	619	91	.279	-2.4	3B(140): -4.1	0.9
2019	TOL	AAA	25	178	153	.367	-1.4	3B(30): 0.1, 1B(7): -0.4	1.5
2019	DET	MLB	25	386	78	.262	-1.0	3B(69): -1.0, 1B(20): -0.2	0.0
2020	DET	MLB	26	206	113	.372	0.7	1B(43): 1.6, 3B(10): 1.5	1.0
2021 FS	DET	MLB	27	600	102	.294	-0.2	1B 1, 3B 0	1.3
2021 DC	DET	MLB	27	571	102	.294	-0.2	1B 1, 3B 0	1.0

Jeimer Candelario, continued

Batted Ball Distribution

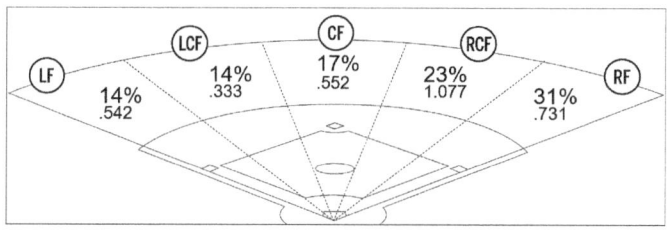

Strike Zone vs LHP   Strike Zone vs RHP

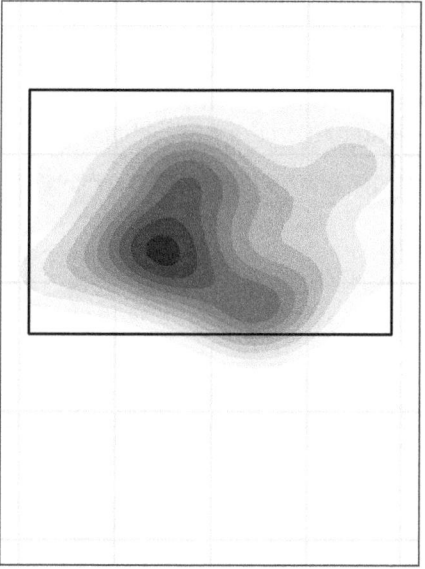

Detroit Tigers 2021

Willi Castro SS

Born: 04/24/97 Age: 24 Bats: S Throws: R
Height: 6'1" Weight: 170 Origin: International Free Agent, 2013

YEAR	TEAM	LVL	AGE	PA	R	2B	3B	HR	RBI	BB	K	SB	CS	AVG/OBP/SLG
2018	AKR	AA	21	410	55	20	2	5	39	28	84	13	4	.245/.303/.350
2018	ERI	AA	21	114	12	9	2	4	13	6	25	4	1	.324/.366/.562
2019	TOL	AAA	22	525	75	28	8	11	62	37	110	17	4	.301/.366/.467
2019	DET	MLB	22	110	10	6	1	1	8	6	34	0	1	.230/.284/.340
2020	DET	MLB	23	140	21	4	2	6	24	7	38	0	1	.349/.381/.550
2021 FS	DET	MLB	24	600	65	25	7	14	63	34	160	8	4	.248/.300/.398
2021 DC	DET	MLB	24	529	57	22	6	12	55	30	141	6	4	.248/.300/.398

Comparables: Tim Anderson, Marcus Semien, Stephen Drew

    Say this about the Tigers: They have a middle infielder type. While all the other contenders are cranking taters, Detroit has a metric pantload of tryhards up the middle who rely on speed, defense, line drive power and absolutely no name recognition or patience. Castro is in the thick of the bunch. His slash line resembled Trea Turner's rookie season, as he slapped every ball between short and third and beat out half the throws. Batting average may be going out of style, but hitting 100 points above the league average never will. He may be more of a second baseman due to the defense, but the bat-on-ball skills will keep him on the lineup card somewhere ahead of the 53 identical players behind him on the depth chart.

YEAR	TEAM	LVL	AGE	PA	DRC+	BABIP	BRR	FRAA	WARP
2018	AKR	AA	21	410	95	.304	1.3	SS(96): 7.5	1.9
2018	ERI	AA	21	114	95	.395	-0.8	SS(10): 0.7, 2B(9): -0.2	0.1
2019	TOL	AAA	22	525	110	.369	0.3	SS(111): -15.3, 2B(7): 0.2, 3B(1): -0.0	1.6
2019	DET	MLB	22	110	68	.333	0.9	SS(29): 1.1	0.3
2020	DET	MLB	23	140	102	.448	-1.4	SS(27): -2.3, 3B(8): -0.6, 2B(1): -0.0	0.0
2021 FS	DET	MLB	24	600	89	.324	1.0	SS -1, 2B 0	0.9
2021 DC	DET	MLB	24	529	89	.324	0.9	SS -1	0.8

Willi Castro, continued

Batted Ball Distribution

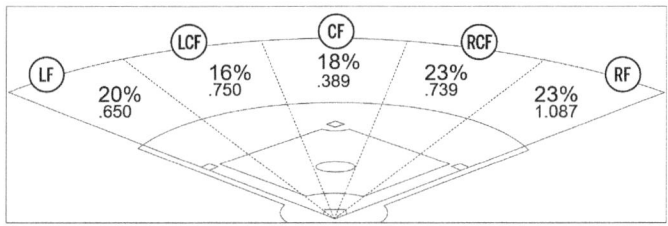

Strike Zone vs LHP   Strike Zone vs RHP

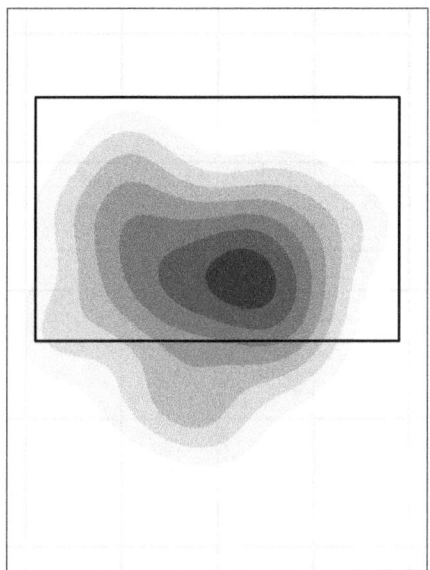

Niko Goodrum SS

Born: 02/28/92 Age: 29 Bats: S Throws: R
Height: 6'3" Weight: 198 Origin: Round 2, 2010 Draft (#71 overall)

YEAR	TEAM	LVL	AGE	PA	R	2B	3B	HR	RBI	BB	K	SB	CS	AVG/OBP/SLG
2018	DET	MLB	26	492	55	29	3	16	53	42	132	12	4	.245/.315/.432
2019	DET	MLB	27	472	61	27	5	12	45	46	137	12	3	.248/.322/.421
2020	DET	MLB	28	179	15	7	1	5	20	18	69	7	1	.184/.263/.335
2021 FS	*DET*	*MLB*	*29*	*600*	*65*	*22*	*5*	*16*	*59*	*54*	*210*	*9*	*4*	*.206/.282/.359*
2021 DC	*DET*	*MLB*	*29*	*448*	*48*	*16*	*3*	*12*	*44*	*40*	*157*	*6*	*3*	*.206/.282/.359*

Comparables: Jeff Baker, Geronimo Pena, Danny Espinosa

Goodrum became the first player in history with two doubles, three strikeouts, five RBI and a walk in a game. This bizarre sampler of outcomes wouldn't have been noteworthy without the three whiffs, which were the story of his 2020, and his entire career, for that matter. Strikeouts aren't awful if you're raking. Goodrum does not rake, although has been known to comb on occasion. Having him on your roster means you have defensive versatility down the lineup, a position type that is getting increasingly common. But only one of them is named Niko.

YEAR	TEAM	LVL	AGE	PA	DRC+	BABIP	BRR	FRAA	WARP
2018	DET	MLB	26	492	97	.312	-1.3	2B(64): 1.0, 1B(37): -0.8, SS(12): -1.4	0.9
2019	DET	MLB	27	472	86	.337	3.4	SS(38): 3.6, 2B(22): -1.9, LF(20): -0.2	1.6
2020	DET	MLB	28	179	74	.276	-1.2	SS(31): 3.6, 2B(11): 0.5	0.2
2021 FS	*DET*	*MLB*	*29*	*600*	*76*	*.300*	*0.9*	*1B 1, SS 2*	*0.3*
2021 DC	*DET*	*MLB*	*29*	*448*	*76*	*.300*	*0.7*	*1B 1, SS 1*	*0.1*

Niko Goodrum, continued

Batted Ball Distribution

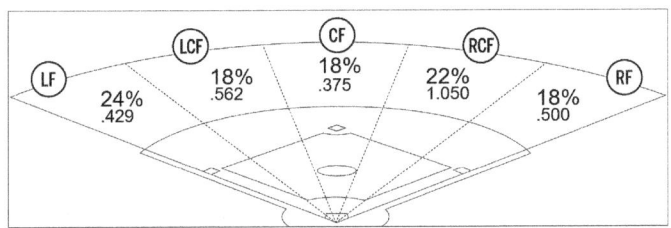

Strike Zone vs LHP   ### Strike Zone vs RHP

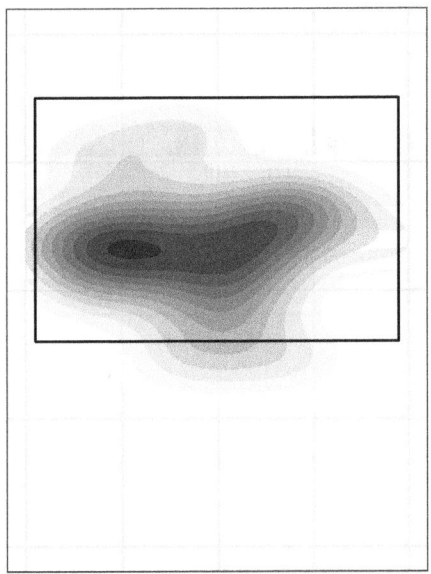

Detroit Tigers 2021

JaCoby Jones CF
Born: 05/10/92 Age: 29 Bats: R Throws: R
Height: 6'2" Weight: 201 Origin: Round 3, 2013 Draft (#87 overall)

YEAR	TEAM	LVL	AGE	PA	R	2B	3B	HR	RBI	BB	K	SB	CS	AVG/OBP/SLG
2018	DET	MLB	26	467	54	22	6	11	34	24	142	13	5	.207/.266/.364
2019	DET	MLB	27	333	39	19	3	11	26	27	94	7	2	.235/.310/.430
2020	DET	MLB	28	108	19	9	0	5	14	7	34	1	1	.268/.333/.515
2021 FS	DET	MLB	29	600	63	25	5	16	56	45	204	10	4	.211/.284/.368
2021 DC	DET	MLB	29	441	46	18	4	11	41	33	150	7	3	.211/.284/.368

Comparables: Ruben Rivera, Reggie Taylor, Michael A. Taylor

    Progression is almost never linear. There are setbacks, slumps and inopportune spells of bad luck that seem inexplicable to us when someone follows a breakout year with mediocrity. We trust in regression to the mean. It's those wretched do-gooders who make four straight years of improvements that throw us into convulsions. Jones' OPS improved by a total 100 points in each of the last four seasons, starting from the lowest of bars. The improvements turned him from hanger-on to capable starter. His whiffs and walks still lag behind the major league median, but with his speed and instincts Jones will remain a useful starting center fielder, and everybody likes those, especially if they don't regress.

YEAR	TEAM	LVL	AGE	PA	DRC+	BABIP	BRR	FRAA	WARP
2018	DET	MLB	26	467	67	.281	4.3	CF(67): 4.0, LF(55): 2.7	0.7
2019	DET	MLB	27	333	87	.304	1.2	CF(85): -7.8	0.0
2020	DET	MLB	28	108	90	.356	0.3	CF(28): -1.9	0.0
2021 FS	DET	MLB	29	600	79	.304	1.0	CF 0, LF 0	0.4
2021 DC	DET	MLB	29	441	79	.304	0.8	CF 0	0.3

JaCoby Jones, continued

Batted Ball Distribution

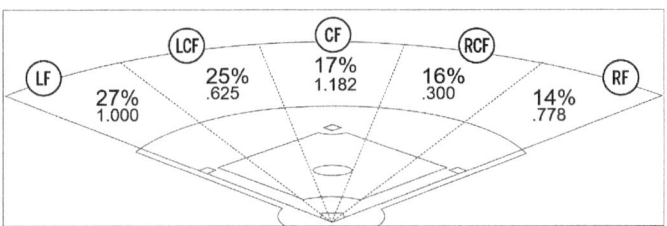

Strike Zone vs LHP   Strike Zone vs RHP

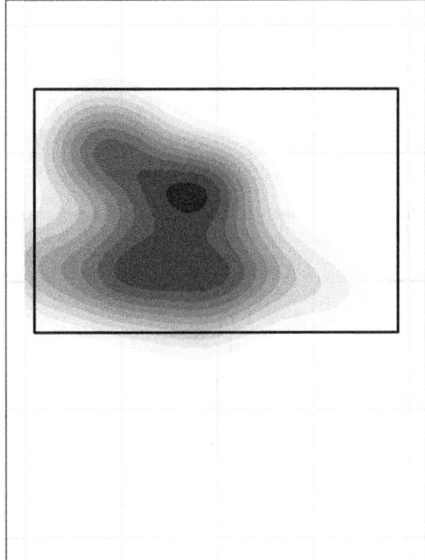

Detroit Tigers 2021

Nomar Mazara RF
Born: 04/26/95 Age: 26 Bats: L Throws: L
Height: 6'4" Weight: 215 Origin: International Free Agent, 2011

YEAR	TEAM	LVL	AGE	PA	R	2B	3B	HR	RBI	BB	K	SB	CS	AVG/OBP/SLG
2018	TEX	MLB	23	536	61	25	1	20	77	40	116	1	0	.258/.317/.436
2019	TEX	MLB	24	469	69	27	1	19	66	28	108	4	1	.268/.318/.469
2020	CHW	MLB	25	149	13	6	0	1	15	10	44	0	1	.228/.295/.294
2021 FS	DET	MLB	26	600	64	28	3	18	70	48	153	2	1	.248/.319/.413
2021 DC	DET	MLB	26	159	17	7	0	4	18	12	40	0	0	.248/.319/.413

Comparables: Brennan Boesch, Jeremy Hermida, George Thomas

Man, that one home run Mazara hit in 2020 was cooked. Turned-and-burned on a high fastball with plus velocity and carry—from Trevor Bauer, no less—with that pristine left-handed uppercut stroke and flung a no-doubter around the right field foul pole and deep into an Ohio night as if he were Jim Thome himself. Ignore the numbers for a second and dream on the tools and skills present, or ignore them for a year or five. Like every great, alluring dream, there are questions that pick at the reality until it falls apart and dissolves. That there was only one home run all year to dream on is only an exaggeration of a career-long trend, where the numbers have never been there and only flashes have emerged that hinted there should be so much more. There probably should be more than there was in 2020 when an already chaotic season was shortened by his own illness, but poor production amid cool highlights has already been ignored too many times with Mazara.

YEAR	TEAM	LVL	AGE	PA	DRC+	BABIP	BRR	FRAA	WARP
2018	TEX	MLB	23	536	97	.298	-1.2	RF(113): -10.2, LF(2): -0.2	-0.2
2019	TEX	MLB	24	469	94	.312	-1.4	RF(101): -5.1	0.1
2020	CHW	MLB	25	149	70	.330	-1.4	RF(42): 1.0	-0.3
2021 FS	DET	MLB	26	600	99	.315	-0.5	RF -1, LF 2	1.2
2021 DC	DET	MLB	26	159	99	.315	-0.1	RF 0, LF 0	0.3

Nomar Mazara, continued

Batted Ball Distribution

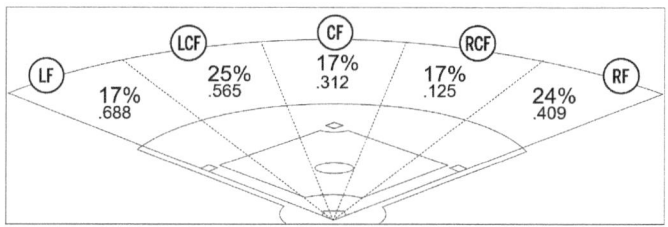

Strike Zone vs LHP   Strike Zone vs RHP

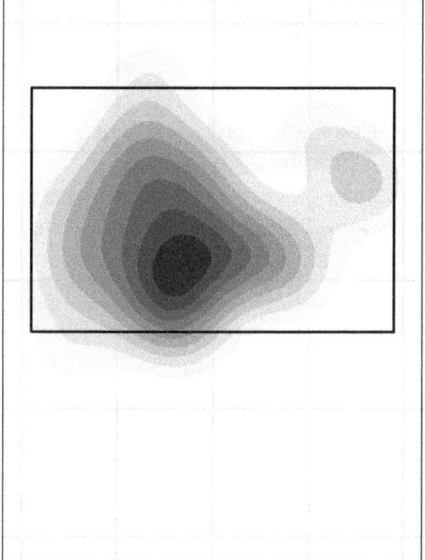

Detroit Tigers 2021

Renato Núñez 1B

Born: 04/04/94 Age: 27 Bats: R Throws: R
Height: 6'1" Weight: 220 Origin: International Free Agent, 2010

YEAR	TEAM	LVL	AGE	PA	R	2B	3B	HR	RBI	BB	K	SB	CS	AVG/OBP/SLG
2018	NOR	AAA	24	228	25	14	1	5	25	23	49	1	0	.289/.361/.443
2018	NAS	AAA	24	30	3	0	0	0	4	2	6	0	0	.357/.400/.357
2018	BAL	MLB	24	220	26	13	0	7	20	16	50	0	0	.275/.336/.445
2018	TEX	MLB	24	41	2	1	0	1	2	3	12	0	0	.167/.244/.278
2019	BAL	MLB	25	599	72	24	0	31	90	44	142	1	1	.244/.311/.460
2020	BAL	MLB	26	216	29	10	0	12	31	17	64	0	0	.256/.324/.492
2021 FS	DET	MLB	27	600	74	23	1	30	85	46	171	0	1	.234/.305/.446

Comparables: Ryan Shealy, Bob Chance, Mike Jacobs

He eclipsed 1,000 plate appearances in 2020 (becoming the 3,658th MLB player ever to reach that plateau), so we feel confident about the following declaration: Núñez is an average major-league hitter. He's got big-boy power and plasters mistakes in the zone. Since the start of 2019, he has more homers than Paul Goldschmidt, Rhys Hoskins, J.D. Martinez and Carlos Santana, despite trailing all of those guys in plate appearances. This would all be cause for excitement if he could play defense like Evan White or Evan Longoria or even Evan Rachel Wood. Unfortunately, he plays defense like a rock-em-sock-em robot actually made out of rocks. His upper and lower halves refuse to work together. They aren't even on speaking terms. He's got brick-and-mortar hands, firm as granite, with less give than Scrooge. He is as DH as DHes come, and on a 2021 roster trying to dish out at-bats to Trey Mancini, Ryan Mountcastle, Chris Davis and Chance Sisco, things were too tight for Núñez in Baltimore (even if he keeps rockin' and sockin' balls over the wall elsewhere). He was non-tendered.

YEAR	TEAM	LVL	AGE	PA	DRC+	BABIP	BRR	FRAA	WARP
2018	NOR	AAA	24	228	129	.356	0.8	3B(38): 0.1, 1B(6): 0.6	1.2
2018	NAS	AAA	24	30	104	.455	-0.5	3B(2): -0.2, LF(2): -0.5, 1B(1): 0.3	0.0
2018	BAL	MLB	24	220	95	.333	-0.8	3B(59): -4.0	0.2
2018	TEX	MLB	24	41	94	.208	-0.2	3B(8): 0.9, LF(4): -0.2	0.2
2019	BAL	MLB	25	599	99	.272	-2.1	1B(24): -1.9, 3B(9): 0.0, LF(1): -0.0	0.6
2020	BAL	MLB	26	216	104	.317	-0.8	1B(28): -3.0, 3B(4): 0.3	0.1
2021 FS	DET	MLB	27	600	96	.285	-1.0	3B 0, 1B -1	0.5

Renato Núñez, continued

Batted Ball Distribution

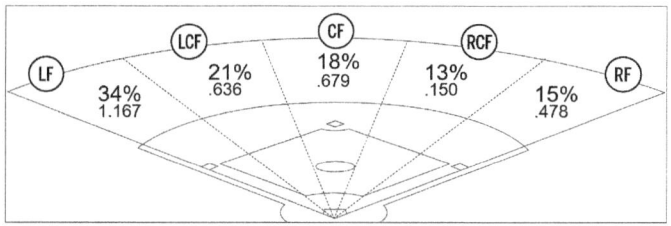

Strike Zone vs LHP   Strike Zone vs RHP

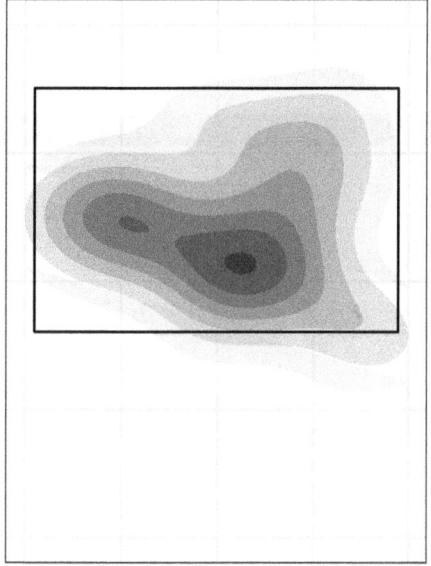

Detroit Tigers 2021

Isaac Paredes 3B

Born: 02/18/99　Age: 22　Bats: R　Throws: R
Height: 5'11"　Weight: 213　Origin: International Free Agent, 2015

YEAR	TEAM	LVL	AGE	PA	R	2B	3B	HR	RBI	BB	K	SB	CS	AVG/OBP/SLG
2018	LAK	HI-A	19	347	50	19	2	12	48	32	54	1	0	.259/.338/.455
2018	ERI	AA	19	155	20	9	0	3	22	19	22	1	0	.321/.406/.458
2019	ERI	AA	20	552	63	23	1	13	66	57	61	5	3	.282/.368/.416
2020	DET	MLB	21	108	7	4	0	1	6	8	24	0	0	.220/.278/.290
2021 FS	DET	MLB	22	600	64	24	3	15	63	48	125	0	1	.234/.306/.375
2021 DC	DET	MLB	22	456	48	18	2	11	48	36	95	0	0	.234/.306/.375

Comparables: Wilmer Flores, Francisco Lindor, J.P. Crawford

　　Paredes arrived in Detroit last summer as part of the Great Call-Up, and in jumping straight from Double-A, found himself overmatched for the first time in his career. There are three other players in the last century who primarily manned third base at 21 years old with Paredes' body type, by height and weight. One was Dayán Viciedo, a reasonable projection in terms of offense productivity. Another is Edgardo Alfonzo, who had far more middle infield prowess. The last is Adrián Beltré, which is a wildly unfair comp so we'll stop right there. Of the three, Alfonzo may be the shrewdest parallel and best-case scenario: modest power, some mobility and a prescient eye for strikes.

YEAR	TEAM	LVL	AGE	PA	DRC+	BABIP	BRR	FRAA	WARP
2018	LAK	HI-A	19	347	126	.274	0.3	SS(59): 3.2, 2B(22): 0.5, 3B(3): -0.1	2.0
2018	ERI	AA	19	155	141	.358	0.3	3B(18): 0.6, SS(15): 0.9, 2B(2): 0.1	1.2
2019	ERI	AA	20	552	137	.298	-2.3	3B(81): -3.4, SS(32): 0.1	3.4
2020	DET	MLB	21	108	81	.280	-0.4	3B(33): -2.4	-0.3
2021 FS	DET	MLB	22	600	90	.277	-0.6	3B -2, 2B 0	0.5
2021 DC	DET	MLB	22	456	90	.277	-0.4	3B -1, 2B 0	0.1

Isaac Paredes, continued

Batted Ball Distribution

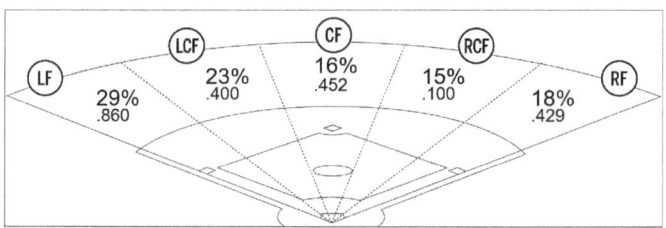

Strike Zone vs LHP   Strike Zone vs RHP

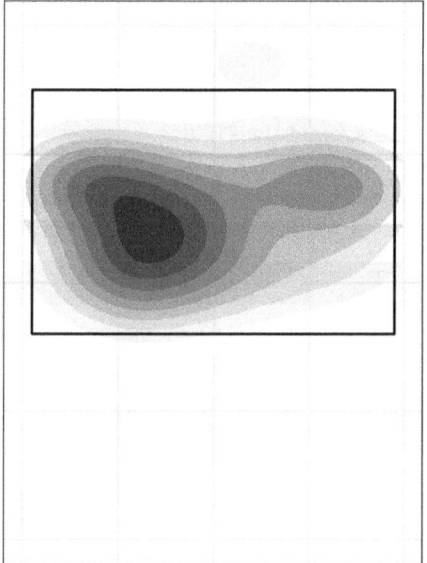

Detroit Tigers 2021

Wilson Ramos   C

Born: 08/10/87   Age: 33   Bats: R   Throws: R
Height: 6'1"   Weight: 245   Origin: International Free Agent, 2004

YEAR	TEAM	LVL	AGE	PA	R	2B	3B	HR	RBI	BB	K	SB	CS	AVG/OBP/SLG
2018	TB	MLB	30	315	30	14	0	14	53	22	61	0	0	.297/.346/.488
2018	PHI	MLB	30	101	9	8	1	1	17	10	19	0	0	.337/.396/.483
2019	NYM	MLB	31	524	52	19	0	14	73	44	69	1	0	.288/.351/.416
2020	NYM	MLB	32	155	13	6	0	5	15	10	31	0	0	.239/.297/.387
2021 FS	DET	MLB	33	600	63	23	1	17	68	40	123	0	1	.252/.305/.394
2021 DC	DET	MLB	33	349	36	13	0	10	39	23	71	0	0	.252/.305/.394

Comparables: Matt Wieters, Ryan Doumit, Terry Kennedy

While PECOTA projected a small decline for Ramos in the 2020 season, the reality was a bit harsher than what our beloved projection system posited. Unfortunately for both Ramos and the Mets, without substantially above-average offensive production, the Buffalo isn't a starting-caliber catcher due to his intolerable defense. (Just one example: a brilliant relay throw could've saved the Mets' August 14 game against the Phillies, but Ramos couldn't lay down a tag at the plate.) Without positive framing numbers, a high-end arm, or other defensive charms, a significant bounce-back at the plate is required to keep Ramos in a starting role, rather than as a bat-first reserve catcher.

YEAR	TEAM	P. COUNT	FRM RUNS	BLK RUNS	THRW RUNS	TOT RUNS
2018	TB	9962	0.2	0.3	-0.2	0.3
2018	PHI	3155	0.1	-0.3	0.2	0.0
2019	NYM	17269	-4.7	-0.5	-3.3	-8.6
2020	NYM	5757	-0.4	-0.5	0.2	-0.8
2021	DET	13228	-3.0	-0.8	-0.1	-3.9
2021	DET	13228	-3.0	-2.6	-0.1	-5.7

YEAR	TEAM	LVL	AGE	PA	DRC+	BABIP	BRR	FRAA	WARP
2018	TB	MLB	30	315	121	.335	-4.4	C(73): -0.8	1.8
2018	PHI	MLB	30	101	122	.408	-2.6	C(23): -0.0	0.5
2019	NYM	MLB	31	524	100	.310	-4.6	C(124): -6.7	1.6
2020	NYM	MLB	32	155	87	.271	-0.6	C(41): -0.9	-0.1
2021 FS	DET	MLB	33	600	94	.293	-0.9	C -7	1.2
2021 DC	DET	MLB	33	349	94	.293	-0.5	C -6	0.5

Wilson Ramos, continued

Batted Ball Distribution

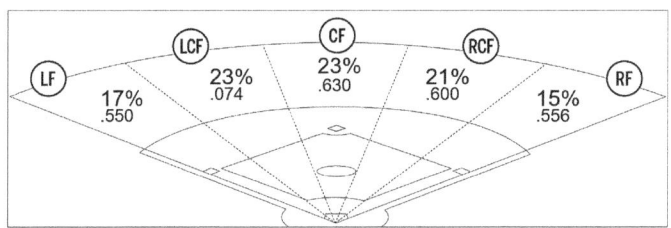

Strike Zone vs LHP   Strike Zone vs RHP

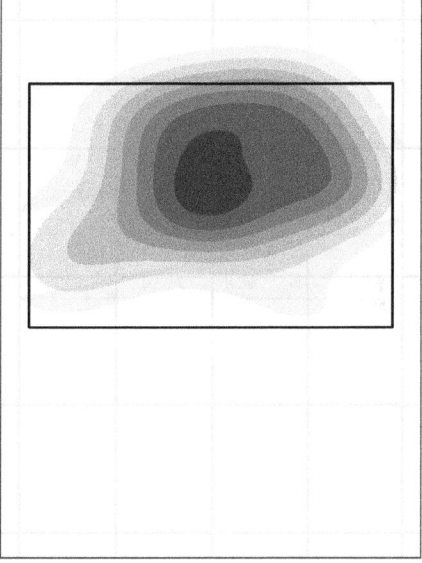

Victor Reyes LF

Born: 10/05/94 Age: 26 Bats: S Throws: R
Height: 6'5" Weight: 194 Origin: International Free Agent, 2011

YEAR	TEAM	LVL	AGE	PA	R	2B	3B	HR	RBI	BB	K	SB	CS	AVG/OBP/SLG
2018	DET	MLB	23	219	35	5	3	1	12	5	46	9	1	.222/.239/.288
2019	TOL	AAA	24	308	50	19	1	10	58	14	50	10	6	.304/.334/.481
2019	DET	MLB	24	292	29	16	5	3	25	14	64	9	3	.304/.336/.431
2020	DET	MLB	25	213	30	7	2	4	14	9	45	8	2	.277/.315/.391
2021 FS	DET	MLB	26	600	67	26	8	11	52	27	133	11	5	.266/.304/.402
2021 DC	DET	MLB	26	424	47	18	5	8	36	19	94	7	4	.266/.304/.402

Comparables: Cecil Espy, Billy Cowan, Greg Allen

A line drive swing isn't always a compliment. For Reyes, it's all he has, and the skill is coming along nicely. Unable to consistently whack the ball 400 feet, he has worked on striving for good contact while using the uncoachable skill of speed to convert the hard-hit singles into extra bases. The plate aggression makes ball four a scarcity, but line drives will play in any league, as hitting enough of those is bound to turn some into long balls. Seasons of 20 doubles and 20 steals—feats that happen about 20 times a season across the majors—are entirely within reach for this former Rule 5 pick.

YEAR	TEAM	LVL	AGE	PA	DRC+	BABIP	BRR	FRAA	WARP
2018	DET	MLB	23	219	63	.277	0.1	LF(34): -3.2, CF(21): 2.2, RF(9): -0.7	-0.6
2019	TOL	AAA	24	308	105	.335	0.4	RF(36): 0.8, CF(31): -0.4	1.0
2019	DET	MLB	24	292	88	.384	-0.4	CF(37): -0.1, LF(21): 2.0, RF(9): -0.2	0.6
2020	DET	MLB	25	213	92	.340	0.7	CF(30): 2.1, LF(22): 0.3, RF(18): -0.0	0.5
2021 FS	DET	MLB	26	600	91	.331	1.4	RF 0, CF 1	1.3
2021 DC	DET	MLB	26	424	91	.331	1.0	RF 0, CF 1	0.8

Victor Reyes, continued

Batted Ball Distribution

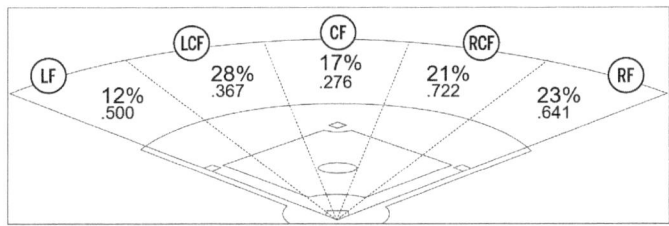

Strike Zone vs LHP   Strike Zone vs RHP

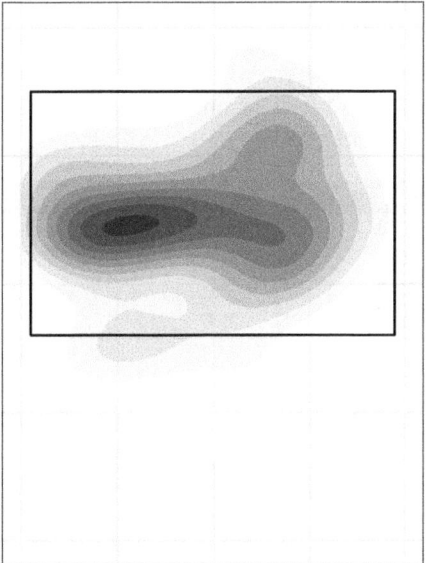

Detroit Tigers 2021

Jonathan Schoop 2B

Born: 10/16/91　Age: 29　Bats: R　Throws: R
Height: 6'1"　Weight: 225　Origin: International Free Agent, 2008

YEAR	TEAM	LVL	AGE	PA	R	2B	3B	HR	RBI	BB	K	SB	CS	AVG/OBP/SLG
2018	BAL	MLB	26	367	45	18	1	17	40	12	74	0	1	.244/.273/.447
2018	MIL	MLB	26	134	16	4	0	4	21	7	41	1	0	.202/.246/.331
2019	MIN	MLB	27	464	61	23	1	23	59	20	115	1	1	.256/.304/.473
2020	DET	MLB	28	177	26	4	2	8	23	8	39	0	0	.278/.324/.475
2021 FS	DET	MLB	29	600	68	25	2	22	74	27	147	1	1	.243/.289/.422
2021 DC	DET	MLB	29	540	62	22	2	20	67	24	132	1	1	.243/.289/.422

Comparables: Jedd Gyorko, Howie Kendrick, Scooter Gennett

Schoop is today's version of Jay Bell, in that he's a second baseman who can crush and you're not sure how old he is or what team he's on anymore. If you bought this book to find out what team Schoop played for in 2020, then money well spent. But for as much as he elevates, he's had trouble leading his team in home runs. In 2016, Schoop hit 25 for the Orioles—and was 22 short of the team lead. The next year he upgraded to 32—and missed Manny Machado's mark by one. Two years ago he belted 23, a paltry eighth on the Bomba Squad. And just when eight seemed like enough before landing on the IL, Miguel Cabrera came out of nowhere with a hot finish to beat him by two. Bell didn't lead his team until his 14th season, so draft Schoop for your fantasy team in 2026 and not a moment sooner.

YEAR	TEAM	LVL	AGE	PA	DRC+	BABIP	BRR	FRAA	WARP
2018	BAL	MLB	26	367	83	.262	-0.6	2B(85): 7.9, SS(2): -0.0	1.1
2018	MIL	MLB	26	134	82	.259	1.0	2B(31): 1.4, SS(15): 1.1	0.5
2019	MIN	MLB	27	464	93	.297	-1.8	2B(113): -5.8	0.3
2020	DET	MLB	28	177	91	.316	1.2	2B(44): 0.6	0.6
2021 FS	DET	MLB	29	600	94	.289	-0.5	2B 1, SS 0	1.4
2021 DC	DET	MLB	29	540	94	.289	-0.5	2B 1	1.2

Jonathan Schoop, continued

Batted Ball Distribution

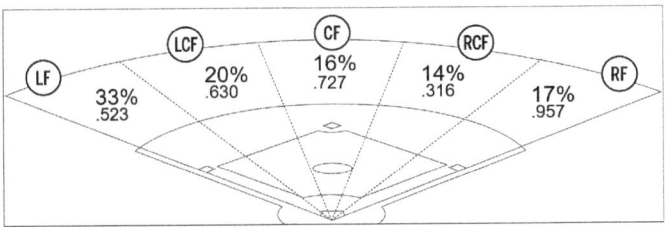

Strike Zone vs LHP   Strike Zone vs RHP

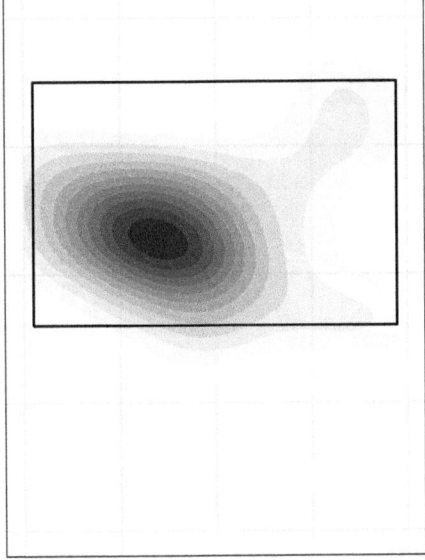

Tigers Player Analysis - 37

Detroit Tigers 2021

Tyler Alexander LHP
Born: 07/14/94 Age: 26 Bats: R Throws: L
Height: 6'2" Weight: 200 Origin: Round 2, 2015 Draft (#65 overall)

YEAR	TEAM	LVL	AGE	W	L	SV	G	GS	IP	H	HR	BB/9	K/9	K	GB%	BABIP
2018	ERI	AA	23	3	2	0	9	9	48	64	7	1.7	6.6	35	42.2%	.361
2018	TOL	AAA	23	3	6	0	17	15	92	120	9	1.3	5.9	60	45.5%	.355
2019	TOL	AAA	24	5	10	0	20	16	98^1	112	18	2.1	9.9	108	39.9%	.346
2019	DET	MLB	24	1	4	0	13	8	53^2	68	9	1.2	7.9	47	36.9%	.347
2020	DET	MLB	25	2	3	0	14	2	36^1	39	8	2.2	8.4	34	45.7%	.320
2021 FS	DET	MLB	26	2	2	0	57	0	50	51	8	2.1	8.1	45	41.0%	.298
2021 DC	DET	MLB	26	10	4	0	67	4	84	85	13	2.1	8.1	75	41.0%	.298

Comparables: Anthony Misiewicz, Nestor Cortes, Jalen Beeks

    Look at a chart of Alexander's pitch usage from game to game or month to month, and you'll find it resembles a plate of spaghetti. He has five different pitches (or six, depending on where you look), and will throw any of them in any count. He can bounce between starts and long relief. He wears number 70 and barely throws 90. He had a mustache in the minor leagues. He's the archetypal crafty lefty (but not Krafty, because if this junkballer had anything that resembled cheese they'd call him Utz).

YEAR	TEAM	LVL	AGE	WHIP	ERA	DRA-	WARP	MPH	FB%	WHF	CSP
2018	ERI	AA	23	1.52	3.75	83	0.8				
2018	TOL	AAA	23	1.45	4.79	93	1.0				
2019	TOL	AAA	24	1.37	5.13	111	1.2				
2019	DET	MLB	24	1.40	4.86	122	-0.2	92.3	54.6%	18.3%	
2020	DET	MLB	25	1.32	3.96	106	0.2	92.0	43.7%	21.9%	
2021 FS	DET	MLB	26	1.26	4.33	102	0.2	92.1	49.2%	20.1%	48.9%
2021 DC	DET	MLB	26	1.26	4.33	102	0.5	92.1	49.2%	20.1%	48.9%

Tyler Alexander, continued

Pitch Shape vs LHH

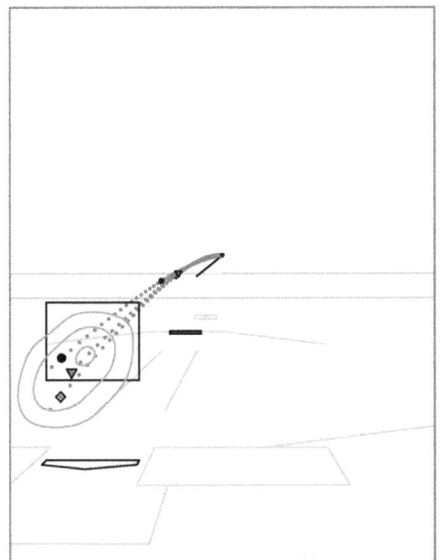

Pitch Shape vs RHH

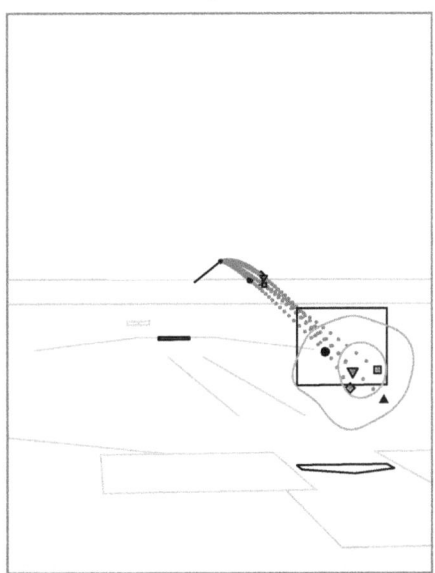

Type	Frequency	Velocity	H Movement	V Movement
● Fastball	22.5%	90.8 [94]	7.2 [98]	-16.4 [96]
☐ Sinker	21.2%	90.6 [91]	12.6 [104]	-18.7 [106]
▲ Changeup	18.0%	84.6 [98]	11.6 [101]	-29.1 [96]
▽ Slider	18.4%	86 [109]	-3.6 [94]	-27.3 [119]
◇ Curveball	19.9%	82.5 [115]	-4.5 [88]	-36.5 [126]

Detroit Tigers 2021

Matthew Boyd   LHP
Born: 02/02/91   Age: 30   Bats: L   Throws: L
Height: 6'3"   Weight: 234   Origin: Round 6, 2013 Draft (#175 overall)

YEAR	TEAM	LVL	AGE	W	L	SV	G	GS	IP	H	HR	BB/9	K/9	K	GB%	BABIP
2018	DET	MLB	27	9	13	0	31	31	170^1	146	27	2.7	8.4	159	29.7%	.259
2019	DET	MLB	28	9	12	0	32	32	185^1	178	39	2.4	11.6	238	34.6%	.310
2020	DET	MLB	29	3	7	0	12	12	60^1	67	15	3.3	9.0	60	37.5%	.310
2021 FS	DET	MLB	30	9	8	0	26	26	150	134	22	3.0	9.4	156	35.8%	.285
2021 DC	DET	MLB	30	9	8	0	27	27	143	128	21	3.0	9.4	149	35.8%	.285

Comparables: Steven Matz, Chris Stratton, Andrew Heaney

You've heard of the Mendoza Line; now feast your pupils on the Boyd Beginning: on August 12, Tim Anderson and Eloy Jiménez kickstarted the game with back-to-back home runs off him. In Boyd's very next start, Anderson and Yoán Moncada did it again. Three starts later, you guessed it, more back-to-back leadoff taters thanks to Jorge Polanco and Josh Donaldson. It was the first time any pitcher had a Boyd Beginning three times in a season. And according to Elias Sports, it was the first time any pitcher did that three times in a whole *career*, and it was Boyd's fourth such Beginning. This homer-prone lefty now joins elite company with Hall of Famer Greg Maddux as pitchers with namesake unofficial starting pitcher statistics.

YEAR	TEAM	LVL	AGE	WHIP	ERA	DRA-	WARP	MPH	FB%	WHF	CSP
2018	DET	MLB	27	1.16	4.39	116	0.2	93.5	48.8%	23.7%	
2019	DET	MLB	28	1.23	4.56	80	3.7	94.2	53.9%	31.4%	
2020	DET	MLB	29	1.48	6.71	140	-0.7	93.3	52.7%	27.9%	
2021 FS	DET	MLB	30	1.23	3.81	91	2.2	93.8	52.4%	28.7%	48.6%
2021 DC	DET	MLB	30	1.23	3.81	91	2.1	93.8	52.4%	28.7%	48.6%

Matthew Boyd, continued

Pitch Shape vs LHH

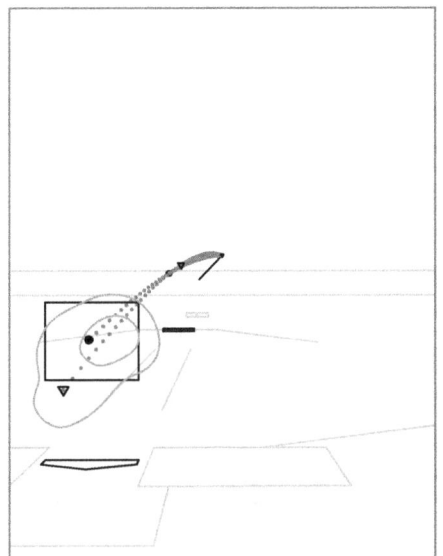

Pitch Shape vs RHH

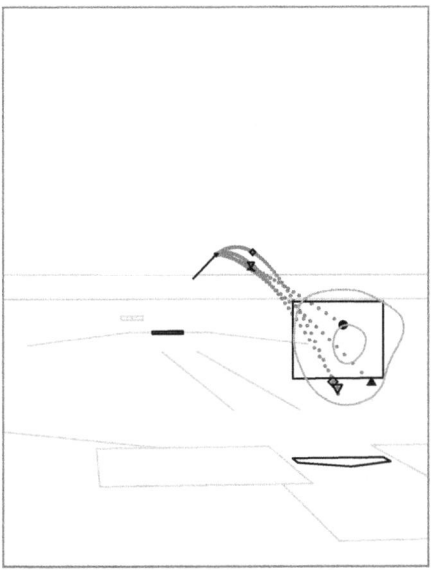

Type	Frequency	Velocity	H Movement	V Movement
● Fastball	49.5%	91.9 [98]	10 [84]	-16.3 [97]
☐ Sinker	3.1%	90.7 [91]	13.6 [96]	-20.6 [100]
▲ Changeup	17.2%	79.2 [77]	14.3 [87]	-33.1 [85]
▽ Slider	22.7%	79.4 [80]	-3 [91]	-41.8 [77]
◇ Curveball	7.5%	74.2 [83]	-11.5 [116]	-58.5 [78]

José Cisnero RHP

Born: 04/11/89   Age: 32   Bats: R   Throws: R
Height: 6'3"   Weight: 245   Origin: International Free Agent, 2007

YEAR	TEAM	LVL	AGE	W	L	SV	G	GS	IP	H	HR	BB/9	K/9	K	GB%	BABIP
2019	TOL	AAA	30	1	2	7	32	2	40	36	3	4.7	11.0	49	41.9%	.327
2019	DET	MLB	30	0	4	0	35	0	35^1	35	5	4.8	10.2	40	37.0%	.323
2020	DET	MLB	31	3	3	0	29	0	29^2	23	1	3.0	10.3	34	36.8%	.293
2021 FS	DET	MLB	32	2	2	0	57	0	50	44	7	4.0	9.8	54	38.2%	.291
2021 DC	DET	MLB	32	3	3	0	62	0	65.7	59	9	4.0	9.8	71	38.2%	.291

Comparables: Tyler Thornburg, Anthony Bass, Jake Petricka

   Cisnero has some odd characteristics that quite don't add up. He's an extreme flyball pitcher who was shelled on contact, yet miraculously avoided the home run. He led the league in innings among relievers who didn't allow multiple dingers. That he's able to get strike three with his heat or his hook is handy; that it adds up to a middle-inning option who keeps it in the ballpark is a wild find. Yes, he had Comerica Park to help, but he also avoided moonshots when he pitched in Minute Maid many moons ago. Swing-and-miss stuff will always play, so we'll have plenty of time to unwrap this riddle.

YEAR	TEAM	LVL	AGE	WHIP	ERA	DRA-	WARP	MPH	FB%	WHF	CSP
2019	TOL	AAA	30	1.43	2.70	88	0.8				
2019	DET	MLB	30	1.53	4.33	109	0.0	98.5	60.8%	26.9%	
2020	DET	MLB	31	1.11	3.03	85	0.5	97.9	63.0%	32.4%	
2021 FS	DET	MLB	32	1.34	4.26	98	0.3	98.1	62.0%	29.9%	46.4%
2021 DC	DET	MLB	32	1.34	4.26	98	0.4	98.1	62.0%	29.9%	46.4%

José Cisnero, continued

Pitch Shape vs LHH

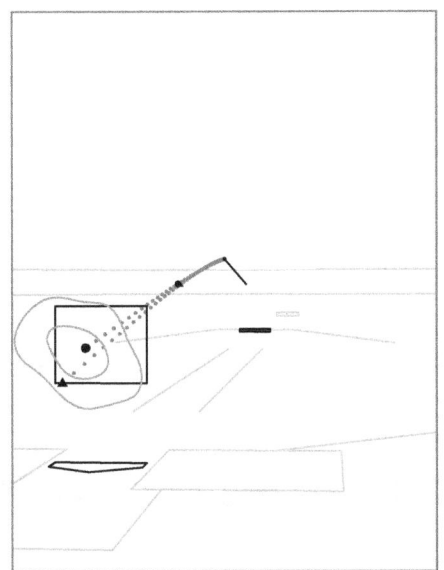

Pitch Shape vs RHH

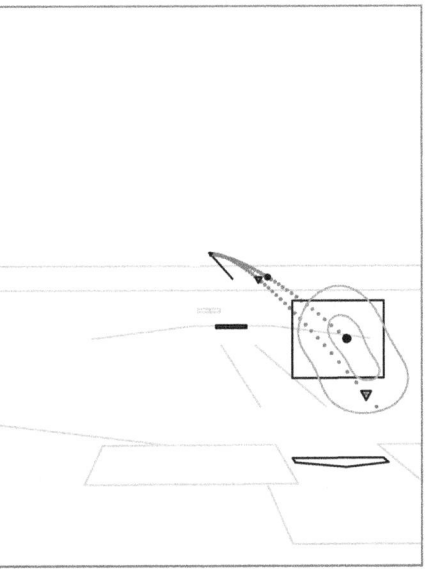

Type	Frequency	Velocity	H Movement	V Movement
● Fastball	58.2%	96.5 [112]	-8.9 [89]	-13.2 [106]
□ Sinker	4.8%	95.3 [115]	-12.6 [103]	-21.3 [98]
▲ Changeup	8.9%	90.9 [122]	-13.7 [90]	-23.3 [111]
▽ Slider	28.1%	86.8 [113]	3.8 [95]	-31.7 [106]

Buck Farmer   RHP

Born: 02/20/91   Age: 30   Bats: L   Throws: R
Height: 6'4"   Weight: 232   Origin: Round 5, 2013 Draft (#156 overall)

YEAR	TEAM	LVL	AGE	W	L	SV	G	GS	IP	H	HR	BB/9	K/9	K	GB%	BABIP
2018	DET	MLB	27	3	4	0	66	1	69^1	67	6	5.3	7.4	57	40.7%	.302
2019	DET	MLB	28	6	6	0	73	1	67^2	62	8	3.2	9.7	73	46.8%	.310
2020	DET	MLB	29	1	0	0	23	0	21^1	20	3	2.1	5.9	14	51.4%	.258
2021 FS	DET	MLB	30	2	2	3	57	0	50	46	6	3.4	8.3	45	45.7%	.285
2021 DC	DET	MLB	30	3	3	3	62	0	65.7	60	8	3.4	8.3	60	45.7%	.285

Comparables: Casey Sadler, Chris Stratton, Jordan Lyles

   It's tough for a relief pitcher to stand out when they come and go like fruit flies. Farmer stands out by being the only active MLB pitcher with the given name George. He blends in by being the Tigers' setup man. He traded some velo on his fastball for some much-needed command, and it paid off with his career-best walk rate; however, away went the strikeouts as well as the utility of his changeup. It may have been an adjustment of the microseason, but becoming a pitch-to-contact strategist is the wrong trend as we head into the '20s. It's as anachronistic as being called Buck.

YEAR	TEAM	LVL	AGE	WHIP	ERA	DRA-	WARP	MPH	FB%	WHF	CSP
2018	DET	MLB	27	1.56	4.15	122	-0.4	96.0	57.6%	26.7%	
2019	DET	MLB	28	1.27	3.72	80	1.1	96.4	49.0%	29.6%	
2020	DET	MLB	29	1.17	3.80	93	0.3	94.5	52.8%	19.9%	
2021 FS	DET	MLB	30	1.31	3.99	94	0.4	95.8	52.2%	26.7%	45.3%
2021 DC	DET	MLB	30	1.31	3.99	94	0.6	95.8	52.2%	26.7%	45.3%

Buck Farmer, continued

Pitch Shape vs LHH

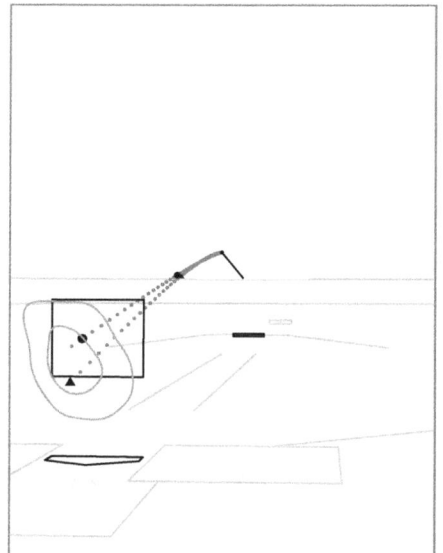

Pitch Shape vs RHH

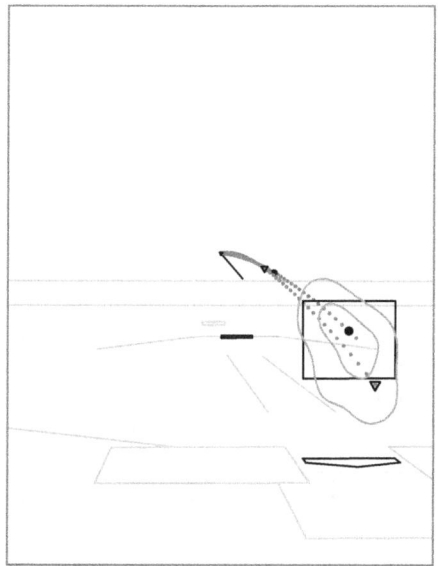

Type	Frequency	Velocity	H Movement	V Movement
● Fastball	52.8%	93.3 [102]	-10.3 [83]	-14.4 [102]
▲ Changeup	32.6%	87.5 [109]	-12.8 [94]	-28.8 [96]
▽ Slider	14.7%	81.9 [91]	2 [88]	-36.1 [93]

Michael Fulmer RHP

Born: 03/15/93 Age: 28 Bats: R Throws: R
Height: 6'3" Weight: 246 Origin: Round 1, 2011 Draft (#44 overall)

YEAR	TEAM	LVL	AGE	W	L	SV	G	GS	IP	H	HR	BB/9	K/9	K	GB%	BABIP
2018	LAK	HI-A	25	0	0	0	2	2	6	1	0	0.0	16.5	11	37.5%	.125
2018	DET	MLB	25	3	12	0	24	24	132[1]	128	19	3.1	7.5	110	44.8%	.289
2020	DET	MLB	27	0	2	0	10	10	27[2]	45	8	3.9	6.5	20	35.9%	.394
2021 FS	DET	MLB	28	9	8	0	26	26	150	145	19	3.3	7.8	130	42.6%	.291
2021 DC	DET	MLB	28	5	6	0	21	21	88.3	85	11	3.3	7.8	77	42.6%	.291

Comparables: Chad Kuhl, Zach Davies, Brett Anderson

   Having your elbow tendons ripped out and replaced by completely different tendons is more painful than it sounds, and the long road back to a professional baseball mound is more treacherous than you may imagine. First things first, Fulmer made it back in one piece. And compared to Lance McCullers Jr., whose surgery and recovery times pretty much overlapped, it went much worse. Fulmer's velocity hasn't returned yet, but his dangerous slider did. He'll continue his recovery in 2021 and work on stretching out and returning to Rookie of the Year form, now wearing the scars of time.

YEAR	TEAM	LVL	AGE	WHIP	ERA	DRA-	WARP	MPH	FB%	WHF	CSP
2018	LAK	HI-A	25	0.17	0.00	38	0.2				
2018	DET	MLB	25	1.31	4.69	104	1.0	97.9	61.0%	23.4%	
2020	DET	MLB	27	2.06	8.78	151	-0.5	94.8	70.5%	19.3%	
2021 FS	DET	MLB	28	1.34	4.19	97	1.7	96.5	65.0%	21.7%	46.3%
2021 DC	DET	MLB	28	1.34	4.19	97	1.0	96.5	65.0%	21.7%	46.3%

Michael Fulmer, continued

Pitch Shape vs LHH

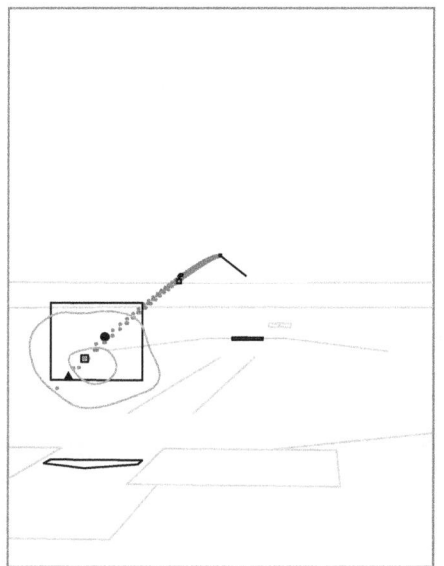

Pitch Shape vs RHH

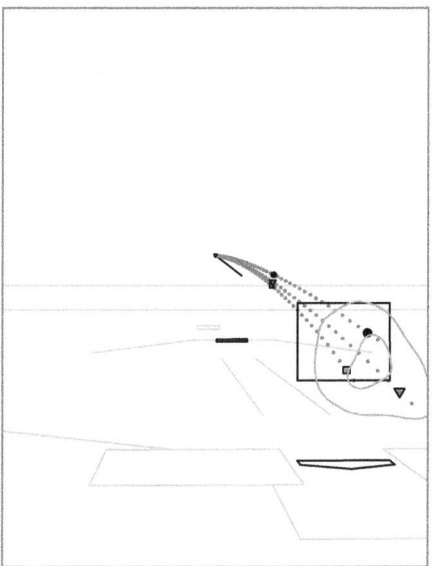

Type	Frequency	Velocity	H Movement	V Movement
● Fastball	28.0%	93.3 [102]	-4.9 [109]	-13.9 [104]
☐ Sinker	34.3%	93.1 [103]	-13.6 [96]	-18.7 [106]
+ Cutter	8.1%	89.2 [106]	4 [114]	-25.1 [97]
▲ Changeup	9.7%	86.8 [107]	-12.4 [96]	-27.2 [101]
▽ Slider	15.0%	86.9 [113]	4 [95]	-28 [117]
◇ Curveball	4.9%	78 [97]	11.6 [116]	-44.9 [108]

Detroit Tigers 2021

Kyle Funkhouser RHP
Born: 03/16/94   Age: 27   Bats: R   Throws: R
Height: 6'3"   Weight: 225   Origin: Round 4, 2016 Draft (#115 overall)

YEAR	TEAM	LVL	AGE	W	L	SV	G	GS	IP	H	HR	BB/9	K/9	K	GB%	BABIP
2018	ERI	AA	24	4	5	0	17	17	89	88	10	3.9	9.0	89	42.2%	.329
2018	TOL	AAA	24	0	2	0	2	2	8^2	8	0	10.4	7.3	7	50.0%	.333
2019	ERI	AA	25	3	1	0	4	4	23^2	16	2	1.1	11.0	29	45.3%	.275
2019	TOL	AAA	25	3	7	0	18	18	63^1	79	3	7.7	9.2	65	53.8%	.396
2020	DET	MLB	26	1	1	0	13	0	17^1	22	3	5.7	6.2	12	48.3%	.345
2021 FS	DET	MLB	27	2	3	0	57	0	50	47	6	6.0	8.5	47	46.1%	.293
2021 DC	DET	MLB	27	1	2	0	37	0	52.3	49	6	6.0	8.5	49	46.1%	.293

Comparables: Dillon Tate, Spencer Turnbull, Rookie Davis

Da Funk wasn't quite ready to bring Da Noize, but that didn't stop the Tigers from corralling him into the bullpen. He's yet to look effective in three seasons above Double-A, which means it's time to reevaluate the starter profile. He found some strike three success with his slider, and that may be enough. Fastball-slider combos never go out of style, not in this house.

YEAR	TEAM	LVL	AGE	WHIP	ERA	DRA-	WARP	MPH	FB%	WHF	CSP
2018	ERI	AA	24	1.43	3.74	85	1.3				
2018	TOL	AAA	24	2.08	6.23	78	0.2				
2019	ERI	AA	25	0.80	1.90	57	0.6				
2019	TOL	AAA	25	2.10	8.53	160	-0.7				
2020	DET	MLB	26	1.90	7.27	120	0.0	97.0	61.8%	23.2%	
2021 FS	DET	MLB	27	1.62	5.25	114	-0.1	97.0	61.8%	23.2%	46.0%
2021 DC	DET	MLB	27	1.62	5.25	114	-0.2	97.0	61.8%	23.2%	46.0%

Kyle Funkhouser, continued

Pitch Shape vs LHH

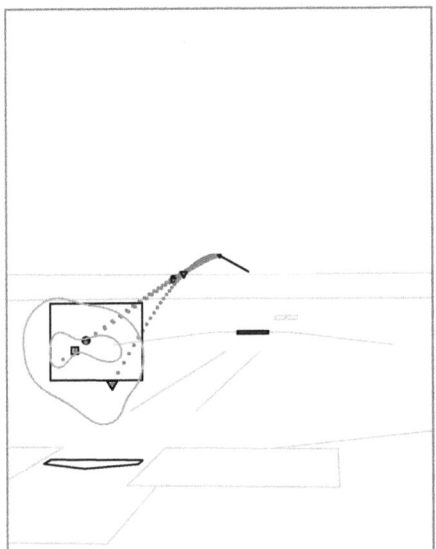

Pitch Shape vs RHH

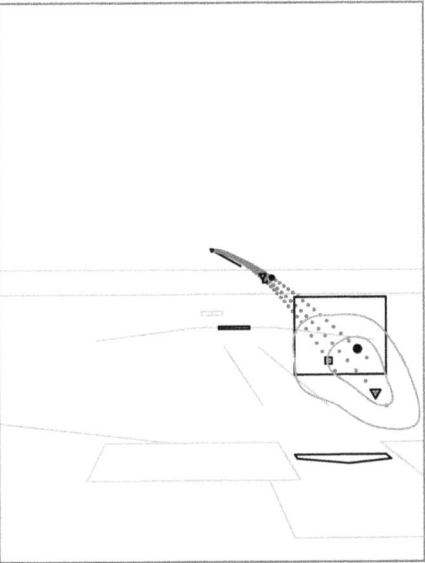

Type	Frequency	Velocity	H Movement	V Movement
● Fastball	28.8%	95.3 [109]	-7.3 [97]	-15.8 [98]
☐ Sinker	32.9%	95.4 [115]	-13.6 [96]	-18.5 [106]
▲ Changeup	6.9%	89.3 [116]	-11.6 [101]	-25.2 [106]
▽ Slider	31.3%	86.4 [111]	3.9 [95]	-32.7 [103]

Bryan Garcia RHP

Born: 04/19/95   Age: 26   Bats: R   Throws: R
Height: 6'1"   Weight: 215   Origin: Round 6, 2016 Draft (#175 overall)

YEAR	TEAM	LVL	AGE	W	L	SV	G	GS	IP	H	HR	BB/9	K/9	K	GB%	BABIP
2019	LAK	HI-A	24	0	0	1	4	0	4	3	1	4.5	13.5	6	33.3%	.286
2019	ERI	AA	24	0	0	1	3	0	4	1	1	0.0	18.0	8	20.0%	.000
2019	TOL	AAA	24	3	0	0	31	0	33^1	26	4	3.8	8.9	33	46.2%	.253
2019	DET	MLB	24	0	0	0	7	0	6^2	9	1	6.8	9.4	7	61.9%	.400
2020	DET	MLB	25	2	1	4	26	0	21^2	18	0	4.2	5.0	12	42.9%	.257
2021 FS	DET	MLB	26	2	2	15	57	0	50	47	6	3.6	8.6	47	42.7%	.292
2021 DC	DET	MLB	26	3	3	15	62	0	65.7	62	8	3.6	8.6	62	42.7%	.292

Comparables: Jake Newberry, Ben Heller, Thyago Vieira

Garcia quickly learned what happens when outs occur under your purview in the Tigers bullpen: You get higher leverage work. After averting crooked numbers by entering bases loaded situations and leaving them clean in back-to-back nights, Garcia was thrust into the closer's role as the clock ran down on the season. He converted four of five, all with some pretty nasty strikeout-to-walk numbers, and not the good kind. The former college closer buzzed down bats in the minor leagues, so his track record of strike threes should diverge from the Todd Jones career arc (though Detroit may be the only team that could stomach it) and into some semblance of late-inning legerdemain.

YEAR	TEAM	LVL	AGE	WHIP	ERA	DRA-	WARP	MPH	FB%	WHF	CSP
2019	LAK	HI-A	24	1.25	4.50	75	0.0				
2019	ERI	AA	24	0.25	2.25	44	0.1				
2019	TOL	AAA	24	1.20	2.97	78	0.8				
2019	DET	MLB	24	2.10	12.15	99	0.0	95.6	51.9%	29.2%	
2020	DET	MLB	25	1.29	1.66	111	0.1	95.7	64.2%	20.1%	
2021 FS	DET	MLB	26	1.34	4.18	97	0.3	95.7	61.6%	22.0%	46.9%
2021 DC	DET	MLB	26	1.34	4.18	97	0.4	95.7	61.6%	22.0%	46.9%

Bryan Garcia, continued

Pitch Shape vs LHH

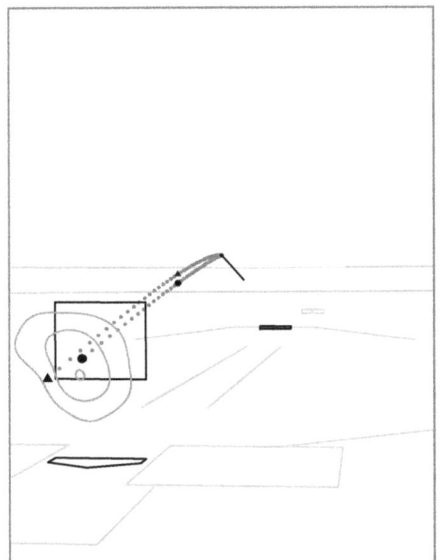

Pitch Shape vs RHH

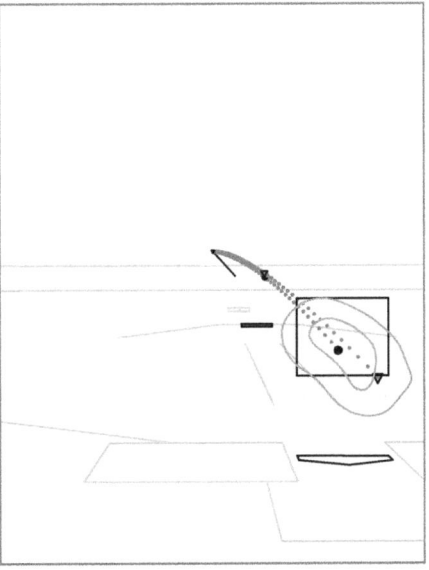

Type	Frequency	Velocity	H Movement	V Movement
● Fastball	64.2%	94.6 [106]	-10.4 [82]	-14.5 [102]
▲ Changeup	13.9%	86.8 [106]	-15.7 [79]	-29.4 [95]
▽ Slider	22.0%	87.4 [115]	2.8 [91]	-29.5 [112]

Detroit Tigers 2021

Rony García   RHP
Born: 12/19/97   Age: 23   Bats: R   Throws: R
Height: 6'3"   Weight: 200   Origin: International Free Agent, 2015

YEAR	TEAM	LVL	AGE	W	L	SV	G	GS	IP	H	HR	BB/9	K/9	K	GB%	BABIP
2018	CSC	LO-A	20	3	4	0	14	14	71	73	5	1.6	7.9	62	32.7%	.312
2018	TAM	HI-A	20	1	5	0	9	9	48	47	2	2.8	8.4	45	40.8%	.326
2019	TAM	HI-A	21	0	2	0	5	4	25	21	2	2.5	9.0	25	32.4%	.288
2019	TRN	AA	21	4	11	0	20	20	105[1]	94	14	3.2	8.9	104	33.8%	.282
2020	DET	MLB	22	1	0	0	15	2	21	25	7	3.9	6.0	14	34.2%	.273
2021 FS	DET	MLB	23	2	3	0	57	0	50	51	9	3.8	7.3	40	34.8%	.288
2021 DC	DET	MLB	23	1	1	0	24	0	45.7	47	8	3.8	7.3	37	34.8%	.288

Comparables: Jonathan Hernández, Tyler Mahle, Pedro Avila

Garcia picked a swell time to be a Rule 5 pick. There's nothing particularly plus about any of his pitches, but he throws them all for strikes, giving him a low but wide ceiling—the bungalow of relievers.

YEAR	TEAM	LVL	AGE	WHIP	ERA	DRA-	WARP	MPH	FB%	WHF	CSP
2018	CSC	LO-A	20	1.21	4.18	90	0.7				
2018	TAM	HI-A	20	1.29	4.50	129	-0.6				
2019	TAM	HI-A	21	1.12	2.16	82	0.3				
2019	TRN	AA	21	1.25	4.44	113	-0.7				
2020	DET	MLB	22	1.62	8.14	160	-0.5	94.5	84.7%	20.0%	
2021 FS	DET	MLB	23	1.45	5.22	117	-0.2	94.5	84.7%	20.0%	46.7%
2021 DC	DET	MLB	23	1.45	5.22	117	-0.2	94.5	84.7%	20.0%	46.7%

Rony García, continued

Pitch Shape vs LHH

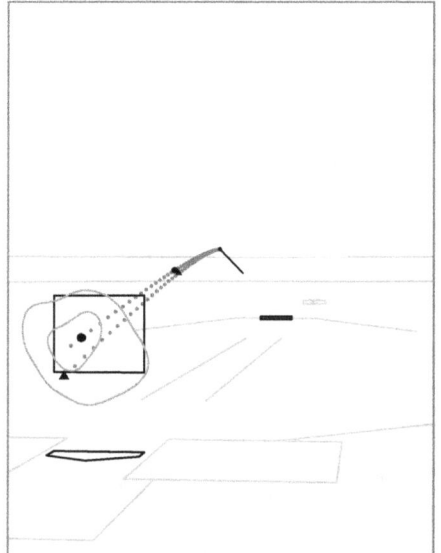

Pitch Shape vs RHH

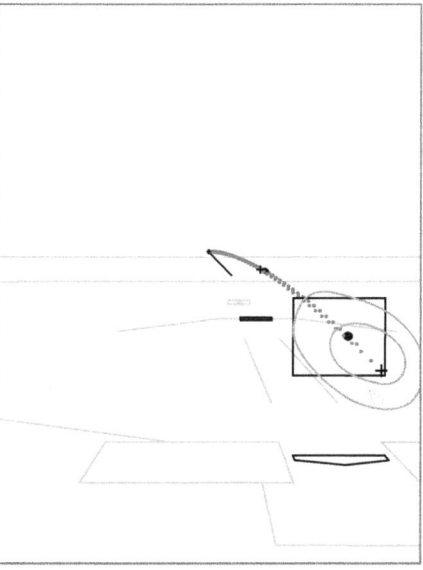

Type	Frequency	Velocity	H Movement	V Movement
● Fastball	63.1%	93.4 [102]	-8.5 [92]	-17.8 [93]
+ Cutter	21.6%	86.1 [86]	3.1 [108]	-28.8 [82]
▲ Changeup	13.2%	88.1 [112]	-13.8 [89]	-26.5 [103]

Joe Jiménez RHP

Born: 01/17/95 Age: 26 Bats: R Throws: R
Height: 6'3" Weight: 272 Origin: Undrafted Free Agent, 2013

YEAR	TEAM	LVL	AGE	W	L	SV	G	GS	IP	H	HR	BB/9	K/9	K	GB%	BABIP
2018	DET	MLB	23	5	4	3	68	0	62²	53	5	3.2	11.2	78	36.2%	.304
2019	DET	MLB	24	4	7	9	66	0	59²	56	13	3.5	12.4	82	29.1%	.319
2020	DET	MLB	25	1	3	5	25	0	22²	25	7	2.4	8.7	22	30.9%	.295
2021 FS	DET	MLB	26	2	2	0	57	0	50	43	7	3.4	10.3	57	32.3%	.284
2021 DC	DET	MLB	26	3	3	0	62	0	65.7	57	10	3.4	10.3	75	32.3%	.284

Comparables: Sam Tuivailala, Keone Kela, Keynan Middleton

The one-time All-Star is starting to pitch like he'd rather have the four-day break in July. Jiménez's lively fastball lost just enough zip and break to turn it into the most depressing of pitches, a Tigers reliever fastball, and he was demoted from the ninth-inning role late in the season. While he's still in his mid-20s, the sample is becoming large enough to expect flashes of untold brilliance followed by devastating sugar crashes. This makes him the archetypal bad-team closer and good-team relief role player, and understanding his streakiness may be the key to a long career.

YEAR	TEAM	LVL	AGE	WHIP	ERA	DRA-	WARP	MPH	FB%	WHF	CSP
2018	DET	MLB	23	1.20	4.31	68	1.4	97.6	67.2%	30.6%	
2019	DET	MLB	24	1.32	4.37	82	0.9	97.0	68.3%	31.6%	
2020	DET	MLB	25	1.37	7.15	141	-0.3	96.2	62.2%	26.4%	
2021 FS	DET	MLB	26	1.24	3.99	94	0.4	96.9	66.4%	29.9%	49.8%
2021 DC	DET	MLB	26	1.24	3.99	94	0.5	96.9	66.4%	29.9%	49.8%

Joe Jiménez, continued

Pitch Shape vs LHH

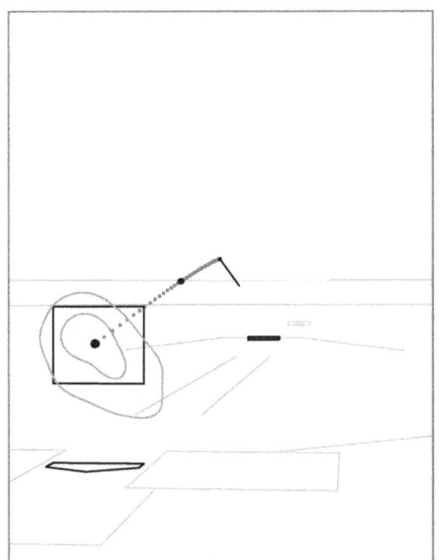

Pitch Shape vs RHH

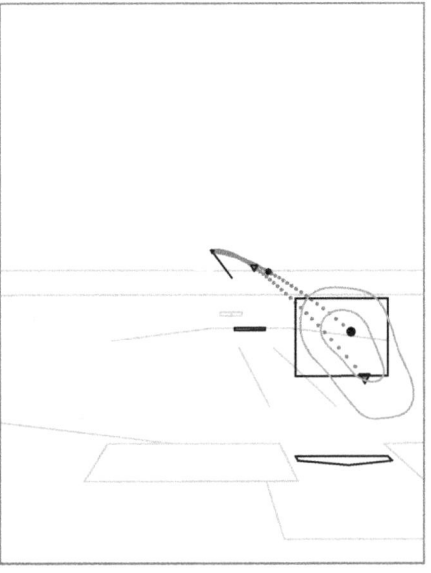

Type	Frequency	Velocity	H Movement	V Movement
● Fastball	62.2%	94.4 [106]	-9.7 [86]	-13 [106]
▲ Changeup	7.2%	89.2 [116]	-14.8 [84]	-26 [104]
▽ Slider	30.6%	84 [100]	5.2 [100]	-33.6 [100]

Detroit Tigers 2021

Casey Mize   RHP
Born: 05/01/97   Age: 24   Bats: R   Throws: R
Height: 6'3"   Weight: 220   Origin: Round 1, 2018 Draft (#1 overall)

YEAR	TEAM	LVL	AGE	W	L	SV	G	GS	IP	H	HR	BB/9	K/9	K	GB%	BABIP
2018	TIW	ROK	21	0	0	0	1	1	2	0	0	4.5	18.0	4	100.0%	.000
2018	LAK	HI-A	21	0	1	0	4	4	11²	13	2	1.5	7.7	10	44.1%	.344
2019	LAK	HI-A	22	2	0	0	6	6	30²	11	0	1.5	8.8	30	45.1%	.157
2019	ERI	AA	22	6	3	0	15	15	78²	69	5	2.1	8.7	76	41.7%	.295
2020	DET	MLB	23	0	3	0	7	7	28¹	29	7	4.1	8.3	26	38.2%	.268
2021 FS	DET	MLB	24	9	9	0	26	26	150	150	24	3.0	8.1	134	39.2%	.294
2021 DC	DET	MLB	24	7	8	0	24	24	126.3	126	20	3.0	8.1	113	39.2%	.294

Comparables: Shawn Chacon, Tyler Mahle, Archie Bradley

   Two years from draft to debut is a short window, though less so for a pitcher with Mize's ability and pedigree. The Tigers made the surprise decision to promote their top prospect early in the season, after a 9-12 start gave them a one-in-six chance of attending 2020's general-admission playoffs. A week earlier (when they were 9-5) or a year later (when they'll be 0-0) might have made more sense. You don't expect rawness from a 1-1 selection, but in seven starts he offered nothing but crudités; at times it appeared as though he was still trying to shake the lingering effects of a nagging shoulder problem from 2019. The fastball darted, the two-seamer ran and the splitter, a powerful, late-biting pitch, hid. But he missed spots and couldn't get ahead, looking masterful one inning and losing his mechanics the next. In an era when teams are overly cautious with their prospects for dubious (economic) reasons, the Tigers really ought to be careful with Mize, who still can be a top-flight candidate. He may not break camp in the rotation, but the minor development sorely needed for a pitcher of this station will help this burgeoning ace start cooking.

YEAR	TEAM	LVL	AGE	WHIP	ERA	DRA-	WARP	MPH	FB%	WHF	CSP
2018	TIW	ROK	21	0.50	0.00						
2018	LAK	HI-A	21	1.29	4.63	91	0.1				
2019	LAK	HI-A	22	0.52	0.88	37	1.2				
2019	ERI	AA	22	1.11	3.20	85	0.8				
2020	DET	MLB	23	1.48	6.99	129	-0.2	95.6	72.0%	23.7%	
2021 FS	DET	MLB	24	1.33	4.64	107	0.9	95.6	72.0%	23.7%	44.7%
2021 DC	DET	MLB	24	1.33	4.64	107	0.7	95.6	72.0%	23.7%	44.7%

Casey Mize, continued

Pitch Shape vs LHH

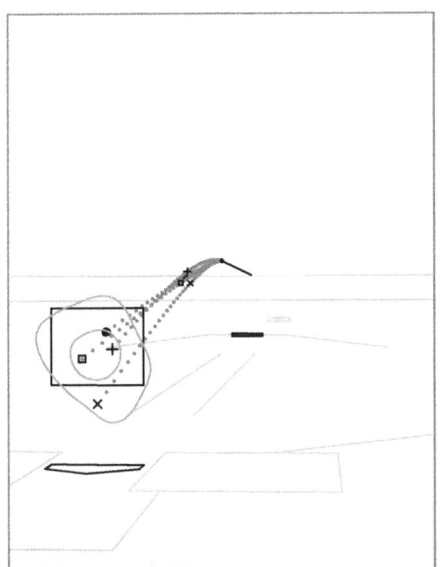

Pitch Shape vs RHH

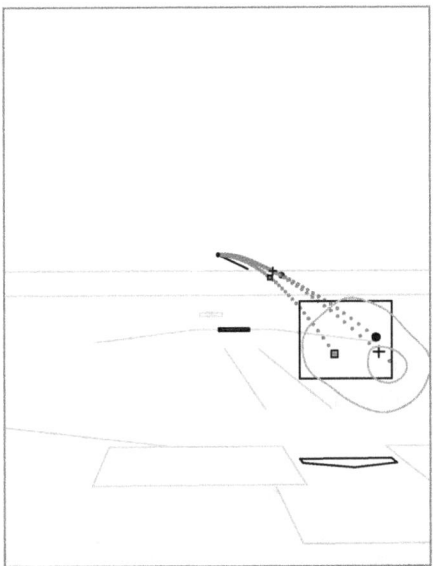

Type	Frequency	Velocity	H Movement	V Movement
● Fastball	25.0%	93.8 [104]	-9.5 [87]	-14.6 [102]
□ Sinker	27.3%	93.7 [106]	-15.4 [83]	-20.7 [100]
+ Cutter	19.7%	88.5 [101]	-1 [81]	-25.9 [93]
× Splitter	17.9%	86.1 [104]	-11.1 [88]	-34 [85]
◇ Curveball	10.1%	80.9 [109]	9.1 [106]	-43.9 [110]

Detroit Tigers 2021

Daniel Norris LHP
Born: 04/25/93 Age: 28 Bats: L Throws: L
Height: 6'2" Weight: 185 Origin: Round 2, 2011 Draft (#74 overall)

YEAR	TEAM	LVL	AGE	W	L	SV	G	GS	IP	H	HR	BB/9	K/9	K	GB%	BABIP
2018	DET	MLB	25	0	5	0	11	8	44^1	46	8	3.9	10.4	51	31.2%	.319
2019	DET	MLB	26	3	13	0	32	29	144^1	154	25	2.4	7.8	125	42.2%	.312
2020	DET	MLB	27	3	1	0	14	1	27^2	25	2	2.3	9.1	28	56.2%	.295
2021 FS	DET	MLB	28	2	2	0	57	0	50	46	7	3.3	9.1	50	44.7%	.289
2021 DC	DET	MLB	28	3	3	0	62	0	65.7	60	9	3.3	9.1	66	44.7%	.289

Comparables: Matt Wisler, Robert Stephenson, Carlos Rodón

If you're a team building a pitching staff by rejecting the orthodoxy of five good starters and five good relievers in lieu of 13 amorphous, useful arms, Norris is going to make your list. He was never able to get quite stretched out following an unfortunate cacophony of maladies, but he had a clean bill of health going out there in multi-inning spurts. In particular, he found increased success when he trusted his changeup and became an extreme groundball pitcher, a stark departure from his previous work. If you're looking for someone who can last five innings every five days, he has the merchandise for it, but he seems to be in a groove going fewer innings with fewer rest days. For someone who's battled every year to stay healthy, you take what you can get.

YEAR	TEAM	LVL	AGE	WHIP	ERA	DRA-	WARP	MPH	FB%	WHF	CSP
2018	DET	MLB	25	1.47	5.68	114	0.1	92.1	52.7%	24.2%	
2019	DET	MLB	26	1.33	4.49	106	0.9	92.9	51.5%	23.1%	
2020	DET	MLB	27	1.16	3.25	78	0.6	94.6	47.6%	27.6%	
2021 FS	DET	MLB	28	1.29	3.94	94	0.4	93.1	50.8%	24.2%	49.3%
2021 DC	DET	MLB	28	1.29	3.94	94	0.7	93.1	50.8%	24.2%	49.3%

Daniel Norris, continued

Pitch Shape vs LHH

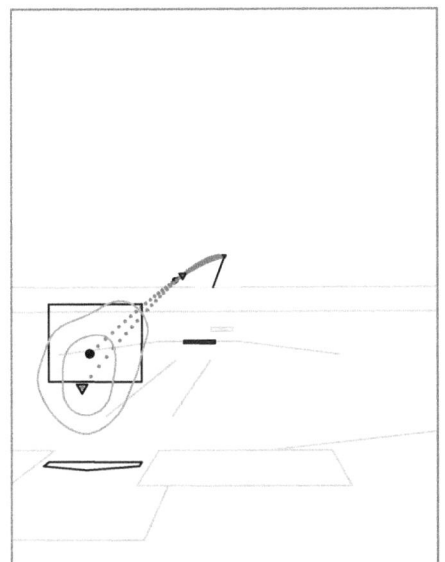

Pitch Shape vs RHH

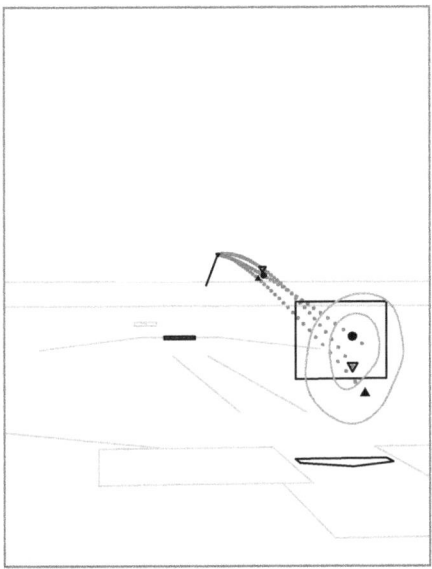

Type	Frequency	Velocity	H Movement	V Movement
● Fastball	47.6%	92.8 [101]	4.6 [110]	-14.3 [102]
▲ Changeup	30.6%	87.7 [110]	11.2 [103]	-32.2 [87]
▽ Slider	21.6%	85.5 [107]	-4.2 [96]	-33.3 [101]

Tigers Player Analysis - 59

Erasmo Ramírez   RHP

Born: 05/02/90   Age: 31   Bats: R   Throws: R
Height: 6'0"   Weight: 220   Origin: International Free Agent, 2007

YEAR	TEAM	LVL	AGE	W	L	SV	G	GS	IP	H	HR	BB/9	K/9	K	GB%	BABIP
2018	TAC	AAA	28	0	2	0	5	5	18²	14	1	1.4	8.2	17	44.4%	.250
2018	SEA	MLB	28	2	4	0	10	10	45²	52	14	2.4	6.5	33	39.6%	.271
2019	WOR	AAA	29	6	8	0	27	24	125¹	125	18	3.1	6.8	95	47.0%	.285
2019	BOS	MLB	29	0	0	0	1	0	3	4	2	3.0	3.0	1	41.7%	.222
2020	NYM	MLB	30	0	0	1	6	0	14¹	8	1	2.5	5.7	9	42.5%	.179
2021 FS	DET	MLB	31	2	2	0	57	0	50	50	8	2.9	7.1	39	43.9%	.285

Comparables: Nathan Eovaldi, Matt Andriese, Justin Germano

Houdini's got nothing on Ramirez, who popped up with the Mets in September and performed one of the great magic tricks of the 2020 season. The well-traveled reliever was asked to serve five innings in relief on September 7, gave up a solo homer to J.T. Realmuto, and never looked back, refusing to concede a run for the rest of the season. Was there some dramatic change in his delivery or velocity that allowed for this dramatic change in his performance from the fringy major leaguer he was over the past several seasons? Nah, there were no tricks up his sleeve. He didn't strike out many hitters or induce ground balls, but lucked into a .179 batting average on balls in play, and a correspondingly shiny ERA. He's likely to regress back to no. 7 starter or long reliever, but at least for a brief moment he was able to be the star of the show.

YEAR	TEAM	LVL	AGE	WHIP	ERA	DRA-	WARP	MPH	FB%	WHF	CSP
2018	TAC	AAA	28	0.91	2.41	79	0.4				
2018	SEA	MLB	28	1.40	6.50	146	-0.7	91.9	40.8%	19.5%	
2019	WOR	AAA	29	1.34	4.74	94	2.5				
2019	BOS	MLB	29	1.67	12.00	143	-0.1	92.0	53.7%	22.2%	
2020	NYM	MLB	30	0.84	0.63	107	0.1	92.1	44.6%	21.3%	
2021 FS	DET	MLB	31	1.33	4.50	103	0.2	92.0	43.1%	20.4%	47.9%

Erasmo Ramírez, continued

Pitch Shape vs LHH

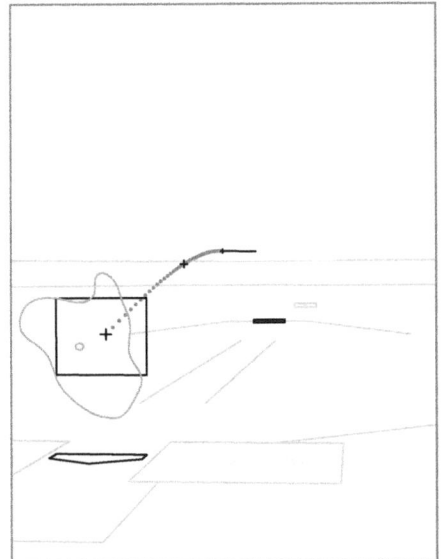

Pitch Shape vs RHH

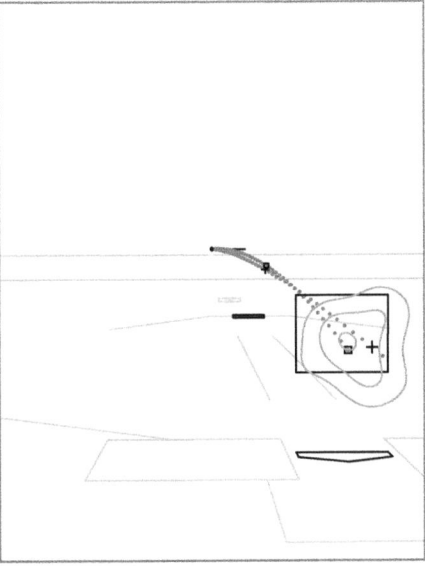

Type	Frequency	Velocity	H Movement	V Movement
● Fastball	3.6%	91 [95]	-8.2 [93]	-16.5 [96]
□ Sinker	41.0%	90.5 [90]	-13.9 [94]	-24.9 [86]
+ Cutter	37.9%	88.1 [99]	1.3 [96]	-20.7 [114]
▲ Changeup	11.8%	83.9 [95]	-11.2 [103]	-28.5 [97]
◇ Curveball	5.1%	79.7 [104]	5 [90]	-40.3 [118]

Detroit Tigers 2021

John Schreiber RHP
Born: 03/05/94   Age: 27   Bats: R   Throws: R
Height: 6'2"   Weight: 210   Origin: Round 15, 2016 Draft (#445 overall)

YEAR	TEAM	LVL	AGE	W	L	SV	G	GS	IP	H	HR	BB/9	K/9	K	GB%	BABIP
2018	ERI	AA	24	3	7	18	49	0	58	47	2	2.9	9.2	59	41.0%	.296
2019	ERI	AA	25	0	0	0	5	0	7	4	1	3.9	15.4	12	57.1%	.231
2019	TOL	AAA	25	6	4	4	48	0	59^1	39	4	3.2	10.6	70	41.0%	.250
2019	DET	MLB	25	2	0	0	13	0	13	16	3	2.8	13.2	19	37.1%	.406
2020	DET	MLB	26	0	1	0	15	0	15^2	19	2	2.3	8.0	14	33.3%	.347
2021 FS	DET	MLB	27	2	2	0	57	0	50	45	6	3.4	9.6	53	39.0%	.294
2021 DC	DET	MLB	27	2	2	0	49	0	18	16	2	3.4	9.6	19	39.0%	.294

Comparables: Phil Maton, Colton Murray, Ryan Dull

The slopball-lovin' Schreiber has Zack Greinke-type stuff from a sidearm angle, but unfortunately has to throw it with John Schreiber's arm. His main contribution to date is a follow-through that makes him look like he's being pulled offstage by an invisible, vaudeville cane. Everyone makes their mark in their own way.

YEAR	TEAM	LVL	AGE	WHIP	ERA	DRA-	WARP	MPH	FB%	WHF	CSP
2018	ERI	AA	24	1.14	2.48	57	1.5				
2019	ERI	AA	25	1.00	2.57	60	0.1				
2019	TOL	AAA	25	1.01	2.28	49	2.2				
2019	DET	MLB	25	1.54	6.23	103	0.0	93.8	61.8%	28.6%	
2020	DET	MLB	26	1.47	6.32	102	0.1	91.7	52.0%	18.2%	
2021 FS	DET	MLB	27	1.28	3.81	93	0.4	92.5	55.6%	22.0%	45.9%
2021 DC	DET	MLB	27	1.28	3.81	93	0.2	92.5	55.6%	22.0%	45.9%

John Schreiber, continued

Pitch Shape vs LHH

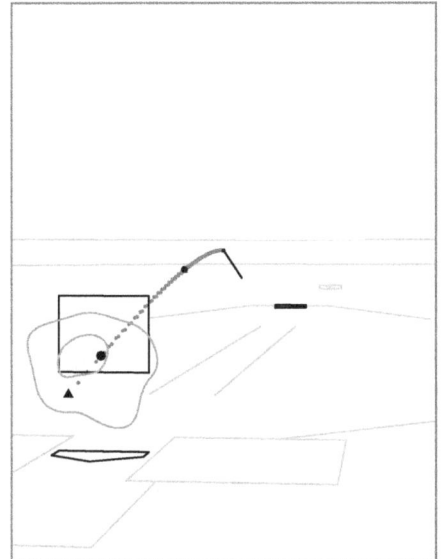

Pitch Shape vs RHH

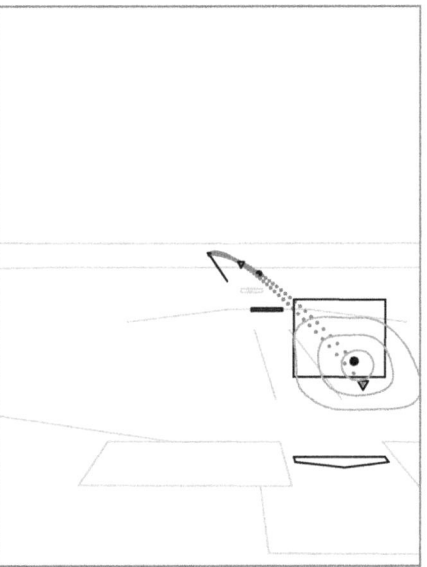

Type	Frequency	Velocity	H Movement	V Movement
● Fastball	50.5%	89.9 [91]	-2.5 [120]	-24.8 [73]
▲ Changeup	13.4%	84.9 [99]	-11.5 [101]	-35.5 [78]
▽ Slider	34.3%	77.6 [72]	13.6 [132]	-39.1 [84]

Detroit Tigers 2021

Tarik Skubal   LHP
Born: 11/20/96   Age: 24   Bats: L   Throws: L
Height: 6'3"   Weight: 215   Origin: Round 9, 2018 Draft (#255 overall)

YEAR	TEAM	LVL	AGE	W	L	SV	G	GS	IP	H	HR	BB/9	K/9	K	GB%	BABIP
2018	TIW	ROK	21	1	0	0	2	1	3	2	0	3.0	15.0	5	85.7%	.286
2018	NOR	SS	21	0	0	1	4	0	12	8	0	1.5	12.8	17	45.8%	.333
2018	WM	LO-A	21	2	0	1	3	0	7[1]	5	0	1.2	13.5	11	21.4%	.357
2019	LAK	HI-A	22	4	5	0	15	15	80[1]	62	5	2.1	10.9	97	39.0%	.294
2019	ERI	AA	22	2	3	0	9	9	42[1]	25	2	3.8	17.4	82	39.1%	.343
2020	DET	MLB	23	1	4	0	8	7	32	28	9	3.1	10.4	37	27.4%	.253
2021 FS	*DET*	*MLB*	*24*	*10*	*8*	*0*	*26*	*26*	*150*	*129*	*22*	*3.2*	*11.0*	*182*	*34.1%*	*.292*
2021 DC	*DET*	*MLB*	*24*	*5*	*4*	*0*	*21*	*17*	*73*	*62*	*11*	*3.2*	*11.0*	*89*	*34.1%*	*.292*

Comparables: Brendan McKay, Eric Lauer, Nick Margevicius

There's not much good news for the minor leagues these days, but one uplifting story is they no longer have to get struck out by Skubal and his massive leg kick on a regular basis. Of all the next-gen Tigers pitchers, his stuff might be as good as or better than Casey Mize's, which explains why they were called up in tandem. The raw left-hander did slightly better than the no. 1 pick, maintaining a double-digit K/9 but getting dogged by far too many orbital white spheres. Still, he improved as the season ripened, and the minor league strikeout artist's debut showed more than enough to put him on the inside track for a rotation spot. You're welcome, minor leaguers.

YEAR	TEAM	LVL	AGE	WHIP	ERA	DRA-	WARP	MPH	FB%	WHF	CSP
2018	TIW	ROK	21	1.00	0.00						
2018	NOR	SS	21	0.83	0.75	61	0.3				
2018	WM	LO-A	21	0.82	0.00	40	0.3				
2019	LAK	HI-A	22	1.01	2.58	68	1.7				
2019	ERI	AA	22	1.02	2.13	49	1.3				
2020	DET	MLB	23	1.22	5.62	137	-0.3	96.9	60.1%	29.5%	
2021 FS	*DET*	*MLB*	*24*	*1.22*	*3.73*	*89*	*2.4*	*96.9*	*60.1%*	*29.5%*	*46.5%*
2021 DC	*DET*	*MLB*	*24*	*1.22*	*3.73*	*89*	*1.1*	*96.9*	*60.1%*	*29.5%*	*46.5%*

Tarik Skubal, continued

Pitch Shape vs LHH

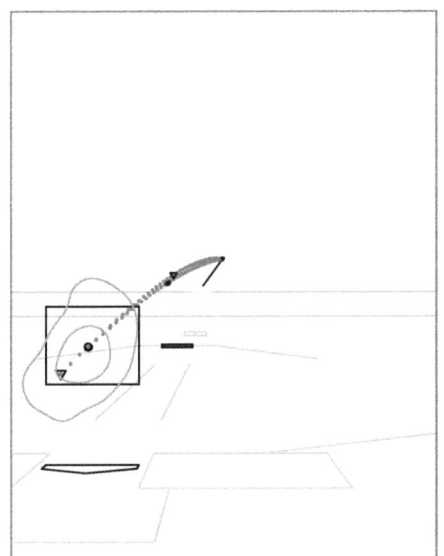

Pitch Shape vs RHH

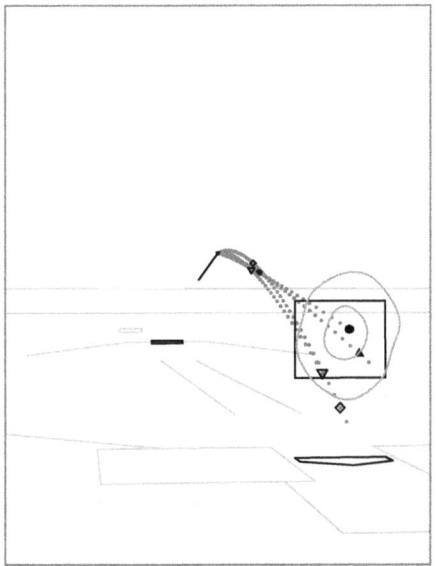

Type	Frequency	Velocity	H Movement	V Movement
● Fastball	60.1%	94.5 [106]	9.8 [85]	-12.4 [108]
▲ Changeup	16.4%	83.3 [93]	8.5 [117]	-22.3 [114]
▽ Slider	15.7%	86.2 [110]	-2.1 [88]	-30.6 [109]
◇ Curveball	7.8%	76.7 [92]	-3.8 [85]	-52.4 [91]

Gregory Soto   LHP

Born: 02/11/95   Age: 26   Bats: L   Throws: L
Height: 6'1"   Weight: 236   Origin: International Free Agent, 2012

YEAR	TEAM	LVL	AGE	W	L	SV	G	GS	IP	H	HR	BB/9	K/9	K	GB%	BABIP
2018	LAK	HI-A	23	8	8	0	25	23	113^1	101	4	5.6	9.1	115	45.8%	.306
2019	ERI	AA	24	0	1	0	3	3	13^1	10	2	2.7	8.1	12	54.1%	.229
2019	TOL	AAA	24	0	3	0	6	5	23^1	25	2	5.0	11.6	30	46.9%	.371
2019	DET	MLB	24	0	5	0	33	7	57^2	74	9	5.2	7.0	45	48.5%	.344
2020	DET	MLB	25	0	1	2	27	0	23	16	2	5.1	11.3	29	53.7%	.269
2021 FS	DET	MLB	26	2	3	12	57	0	50	47	6	5.4	9.4	52	48.3%	.303
2021 DC	DET	MLB	26	3	3	12	62	0	59	55	7	5.4	9.4	61	48.3%	.303

Comparables: Thomas Pannone, Conner Menez, Matt Hall

After opening some games in 2019 in cringeworthy fashion, Soto pared down his options, cleaned up his delivery and stuck with two pitches in late innings. Moving to a slide-step delivery helped add some racing stripes to his sinker, and he now slings it harder than any left-hander, scraping triple digits. The slider is the simple baguette to the sinker's entrée. He tosses a few too many balls four to make him comfortable as a ninth-inning hurler, but having this Soto around certainly adds a dynamic alternative as the game reaches its final courses.

YEAR	TEAM	LVL	AGE	WHIP	ERA	DRA-	WARP	MPH	FB%	WHF	CSP
2018	LAK	HI-A	23	1.51	4.45	83	1.7				
2019	ERI	AA	24	1.05	2.02	76	0.2				
2019	TOL	AAA	24	1.63	6.94	106	0.3				
2019	DET	MLB	24	1.86	5.77	156	-1.3	97.9	70.7%	20.0%	
2020	DET	MLB	25	1.26	4.30	79	0.5	99.0	79.7%	28.8%	
2021 FS	DET	MLB	26	1.54	4.88	107	0.0	98.3	73.8%	23.1%	50.3%
2021 DC	DET	MLB	26	1.54	4.88	107	0.1	98.3	73.8%	23.1%	50.3%

Gregory Soto, continued

Pitch Shape vs LHH

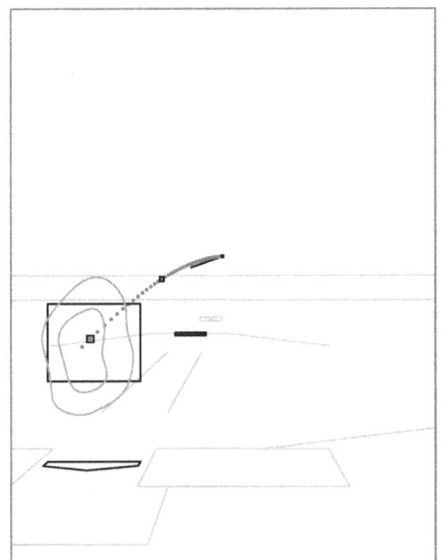

Pitch Shape vs RHH

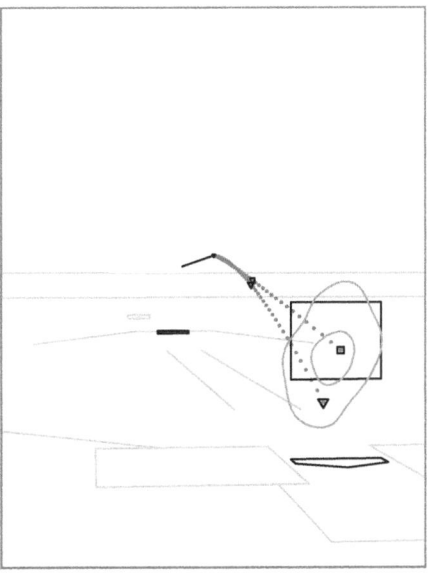

Type	Frequency	Velocity	H Movement	V Movement
● Fastball	6.9%	97.1 [114]	5.4 [106]	-13.5 [105]
□ Sinker	72.8%	97.4 [125]	12.9 [101]	-16.1 [114]
▽ Slider	20.3%	87.8 [117]	-3.4 [93]	-28.3 [116]

Detroit Tigers 2021

Spencer Turnbull RHP
Born: 09/18/92   Age: 28   Bats: R   Throws: R
Height: 6'3"   Weight: 211   Origin: Round 2, 2014 Draft (#63 overall)

YEAR	TEAM	LVL	AGE	W	L	SV	G	GS	IP	H	HR	BB/9	K/9	K	GB%	BABIP
2018	TIW	ROK	25	0	0	0	1	1	2^2	1	0	10.1	10.1	3	50.0%	.167
2018	LAK	HI-A	25	0	0	0	1	1	4^2	2	0	0.0	11.6	6	40.0%	.200
2018	ERI	AA	25	4	7	0	19	19	98^2	92	4	3.6	9.6	105	54.3%	.332
2018	TOL	AAA	25	1	1	0	2	2	13^1	8	0	2.0	12.8	19	40.0%	.296
2018	DET	MLB	25	0	2	0	4	3	16^1	17	1	2.2	8.3	15	48.0%	.327
2019	TOL	AAA	26	0	0	0	1	1	3^2	1	0	0.0	17.2	7	60.0%	.200
2019	DET	MLB	26	3	17	0	30	30	148^1	154	14	3.6	8.9	146	48.0%	.333
2020	DET	MLB	27	4	4	0	11	11	56^2	47	2	4.6	8.1	51	48.8%	.288
2021 FS	DET	MLB	28	9	8	0	26	26	150	140	18	4.2	9.1	150	49.0%	.297
2021 DC	DET	MLB	28	9	8	0	27	27	145.7	136	18	4.2	9.1	146	49.0%	.297

Comparables: Kevin Gausman, Erick Fedde, Zach Davies

Can't give up home runs if you keep walking batters, says the meme of the smiling man pointing to his head. With some outrageously bendy pitches, Turnbull is turning into an effectively wild type, hold the effectively. His 14:1 walk-to-home run ratio isn't unprecedented, as a list of such pitchers is extensive, but the entire list is pretty much relievers. You have to go back to Brandon Duckworth in 2001 to find a starter who gave up 14 times as many free passes as long balls in a season. Maybe it's just that the batters know to lay off the pitches. Maybe it's as simple as having an animal in the last name. The science is inconclusive.

YEAR	TEAM	LVL	AGE	WHIP	ERA	DRA-	WARP	MPH	FB%	WHF	CSP
2018	TIW	ROK	25	1.50	0.00						
2018	LAK	HI-A	25	0.43	0.00	59	0.1				
2018	ERI	AA	25	1.34	4.47	79	1.8				
2018	TOL	AAA	25	0.82	2.02	56	0.4				
2018	DET	MLB	25	1.29	6.06	111	0.1	96.0	63.5%	21.2%	
2019	TOL	AAA	26	0.27	0.00	30	0.2				
2019	DET	MLB	26	1.44	4.61	106	0.9	95.9	64.8%	24.7%	
2020	DET	MLB	27	1.34	3.97	87	0.9	96.4	66.0%	28.3%	
2021 FS	DET	MLB	28	1.41	4.47	101	1.3	96.1	65.2%	25.8%	46.0%
2021 DC	DET	MLB	28	1.41	4.47	101	1.3	96.1	65.2%	25.8%	46.0%

Spencer Turnbull, continued

Pitch Shape vs LHH

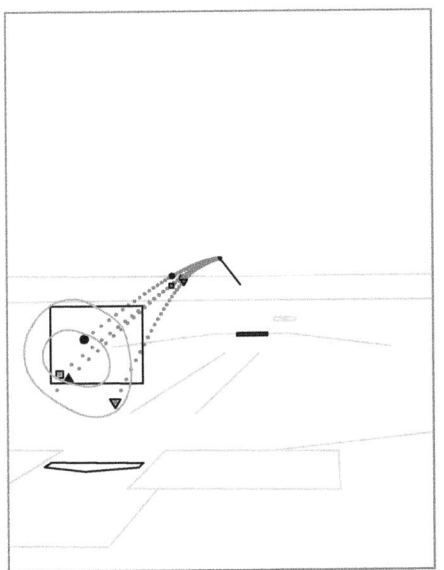

Pitch Shape vs RHH

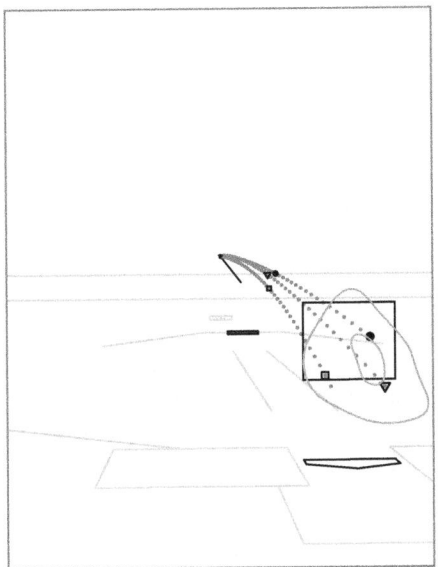

Type	Frequency	Velocity	H Movement	V Movement
● Fastball	45.0%	93.9 [104]	-1.9 [123]	-17.6 [93]
☐ Sinker	20.8%	95 [113]	-13.8 [95]	-21.6 [97]
▲ Changeup	9.0%	87.3 [108]	-15.5 [80]	-31.3 [89]
▽ Slider	20.7%	85.5 [107]	6 [103]	-34.3 [99]
◇ Curveball	4.1%	79.6 [104]	9.3 [107]	-49.5 [98]

Detroit Tigers 2021

José Ureña RHP
Born: 09/12/91   Age: 29   Bats: R   Throws: R
Height: 6'2"   Weight: 208   Origin: International Free Agent, 2008

YEAR	TEAM	LVL	AGE	W	L	SV	G	GS	IP	H	HR	BB/9	K/9	K	GB%	BABIP
2018	MIA	MLB	26	9	12	0	31	31	174	155	19	2.6	6.7	130	49.3%	.275
2019	MIA	MLB	27	4	10	3	24	13	84²	99	13	2.8	6.6	62	48.7%	.325
2020	MIA	MLB	28	0	3	0	5	5	23¹	22	4	5.0	5.8	15	45.9%	.257
2021 FS	DET	MLB	29	9	9	0	26	26	150	152	20	3.6	7.0	116	47.0%	.292
2021 DC	DET	MLB	29	6	6	0	41	12	88.3	89	12	3.6	7.0	68	47.0%	.292

Comparables: Trevor Williams, Mike Foltynewicz, Matt Harrison

Ureña was a late scratch from his planned first start due to a positive COVID test, in one of the earliest signs of the burgeoning outbreak in the Marlins clubhouse. Despite early media reports that he was asymptomatic, he was not ready to come back when the Marlins resumed play and ultimately missed nearly six weeks with the virus. The bad luck didn't end there, either; he got drilled by a comebacker on the very last day of the regular season and broke his pitching arm, taking him out of the playoffs. When able to take the mound, Ureña was the same pitcher he's always been: a flamethrower who just doesn't have enough else going for him to be more than a back-end starter. The capper on a terrible, horrible, no good, very bad year? The Marlins designated him for assignment upon acquiring Adam Cimber and he latched on with the Tigers.

YEAR	TEAM	LVL	AGE	WHIP	ERA	DRA-	WARP	MPH	FB%	WHF	CSP
2018	MIA	MLB	26	1.18	3.98	89	2.6	97.6	58.8%	20.4%	
2019	MIA	MLB	27	1.48	5.21	117	0.0	97.7	63.1%	21.3%	
2020	MIA	MLB	28	1.50	5.40	128	-0.1	96.9	60.9%	27.1%	
2021 FS	DET	MLB	29	1.42	4.71	106	0.9	97.5	60.9%	22.0%	46.0%
2021 DC	DET	MLB	29	1.42	4.71	106	0.5	97.5	60.9%	22.0%	46.0%

José Ureña, continued

Pitch Shape vs LHH

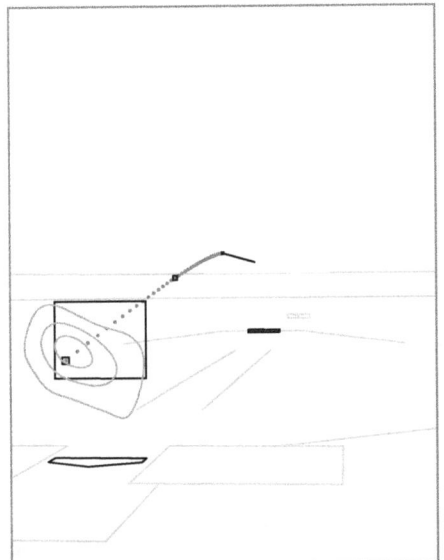

Pitch Shape vs RHH

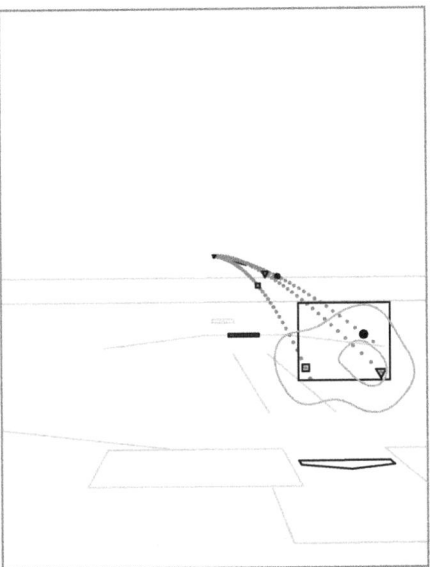

Type	Frequency	Velocity	H Movement	V Movement
● Fastball	18.4%	95.8 [110]	-8.8 [90]	-14.7 [101]
□ Sinker	42.4%	95.4 [115]	-14.2 [91]	-20.9 [99]
▲ Changeup	6.8%	90.5 [121]	-12.2 [98]	-20.4 [119]
▽ Slider	32.3%	85.8 [108]	1.8 [87]	-29.4 [113]

PLAYER COMMENTS WITHOUT GRAPHS

Akil Baddoo CF
Born: 08/16/98 Age: 22 Bats: L Throws: L
Height: 6'1" Weight: 210 Origin: Round 2, 2016 Draft (#74 overall)

YEAR	TEAM	LVL	AGE	PA	R	2B	3B	HR	RBI	BB	K	SB	CS	AVG/OBP/SLG
2018	CR	LO-A	19	517	83	22	11	11	40	74	124	24	5	.243/.351/.419
2019	FTM	HI-A	20	131	15	3	3	4	9	12	39	6	2	.214/.290/.393
2021 FS	DET	MLB	22	600	57	22	8	12	55	53	194	11	4	.202/.279/.340
2021 DC	DET	MLB	22	66	6	2	0	1	6	5	21	0	1	.202/.279/.340

Comparables: Joe Benson, Clint Frazier, Aaron Hicks

The third-overall pick in the Rule 5 draft, Baddoo struggled mightily in High-A to close out the 2019 season, and there's little to suggest he'll survive a full season in the majors. Of course, the Tigers' entire outfield is populated by players who probably don't belong in the big leaugues, so at least Baddoo is their type.

YEAR	TEAM	LVL	AGE	PA	DRC+	BABIP	BRR	FRAA	WARP
2018	CR	LO-A	19	517	116	.311	4.7	CF(97): -12.1, LF(3): 0.1	1.0
2019	FTM	HI-A	20	131	89	.280	1.6	CF(21): -2.7, LF(6): -0.2	0.1
2021 FS	DET	MLB	22	600	67	.293	1.7	CF -3, LF 0	-0.8
2021 DC	DET	MLB	22	66	67	.293	0.2	CF 0	-0.1

Daz Cameron CF

Born: 01/15/97 Age: 24 Bats: R Throws: R
Height: 6'2" Weight: 185 Origin: Round 1, 2015 Draft (#37 overall)

YEAR	TEAM	LVL	AGE	PA	R	2B	3B	HR	RBI	BB	K	SB	CS	AVG/OBP/SLG
2018	LAK	HI-A	21	246	35	9	3	3	20	25	69	10	4	.259/.346/.370
2018	ERI	AA	21	226	32	12	5	5	35	25	53	12	5	.285/.367/.470
2018	TOL	AAA	21	62	8	4	1	0	6	2	15	2	2	.211/.246/.316
2019	TOL	AAA	22	528	68	22	6	13	43	62	152	17	8	.214/.330/.377
2020	DET	MLB	23	59	4	2	1	0	3	2	19	1	0	.193/.220/.263
2021 FS	DET	MLB	24	600	60	22	8	13	55	51	204	14	7	.205/.285/.351
2021 DC	DET	MLB	24	157	15	5	2	3	14	13	53	3	2	.205/.285/.351

Comparables: Anthony Gose, Michael Saunders, Dalton Pompey

Father-son comparisons tend to evaporate when the progeny eclipses the progenitor. Cody Bellinger outdid Clay's career in about two months. Bobby Bonds was memory-holed by Barry. The Junior is the peak-performance Griffey. But the other way around? Tony Gwynn, Jr. was always chasing dad. Terry Francona didn't have the playing career of his father, and as penance, people call him Tito. Now that Cameron has debuted, it's important to note Mike beat him to the majors according to age by exactly 53 weeks. It's hard to envision the younger Cameron finishing with 1,700 career hits and nearly 300 home runs like Pops, especially since the plate skills remain a yellow flag, but it's easy to see him patrol center field and time warp back to the early 2000s Mariners.

YEAR	TEAM	LVL	AGE	PA	DRC+	BABIP	BRR	FRAA	WARP
2018	LAK	HI-A	21	246	117	.366	2.5	CF(38): 1.9, RF(18): 0.9	1.2
2018	ERI	AA	21	226	123	.366	3.4	CF(34): -7.0, RF(16): 1.5	0.7
2018	TOL	AAA	21	62	55	.279	0.7	CF(14): 0.3, RF(1): 0.0	-0.1
2019	TOL	AAA	22	528	86	.291	2.4	CF(93): -1.0, RF(19): 5.4	1.3
2020	DET	MLB	23	59	68	.289	0.1	RF(16): 0.5	-0.1
2021 FS	DET	MLB	24	600	75	.303	2.2	RF 8, CF 0	0.9
2021 DC	DET	MLB	24	157	75	.303	0.6	RF 2	0.1

Detroit Tigers 2021

Harold Castro 3B
Born: 11/30/93   Age: 27   Bats: L   Throws: R
Height: 5'10"   Weight: 151   Origin: International Free Agent, 2011

YEAR	TEAM	LVL	AGE	PA	R	2B	3B	HR	RBI	BB	K	SB	CS	AVG/OBP/SLG
2018	ERI	AA	24	116	10	5	0	0	10	4	21	2	1	.282/.310/.327
2018	TOL	AAA	24	251	24	8	0	2	19	5	47	3	3	.257/.270/.315
2018	DET	MLB	24	10	2	0	0	0	0	0	2	1	0	.300/.300/.300
2019	TOL	AAA	25	134	20	5	1	4	25	9	26	1	3	.328/.371/.484
2019	DET	MLB	25	369	30	10	4	5	38	9	86	4	2	.291/.305/.384
2020	DET	MLB	26	54	6	4	0	0	3	5	11	0	0	.347/.407/.429
2021 FS	DET	MLB	27	600	58	27	4	10	57	22	137	6	4	.255/.289/.373
2021 DC	DET	MLB	27	271	26	12	2	4	25	10	62	2	2	.255/.289/.373

Comparables: Bo Hart, Jerry Buchek, Fred Manrique

If Castro were the main protagonist in *Where's Waldo* books, kids would stop reading them in sheer frustration; he starts everywhere and is impossible to find. He missed a month with a lame hammy in an already teensy season, and still managed to start a game at every position except second base. It's entirely possible he's writing himself into the lineup with the purple crayon. He lacks the requisite power or speed to secure substantial lineup card placement, but Hittin' Harold's batting average hasn't lied to him yet.

YEAR	TEAM	LVL	AGE	PA	DRC+	BABIP	BRR	FRAA	WARP
2018	ERI	AA	24	116	78	.344	0.1	2B(14): -1.6, 3B(8): 0.9, LF(3): 0.0	-0.3
2018	TOL	AAA	24	251	67	.309	1.0	3B(30): -0.1, SS(22): -1.7, 2B(12): -2.1	-0.7
2018	DET	MLB	24	10	79	.375	-0.1	SS(4): 0.1, 2B(2): 0.0	0.0
2019	TOL	AAA	25	134	123	.387	1.6	2B(23): -1.0, 1B(2): 0.1, 3B(2): 0.1	0.9
2019	DET	MLB	25	369	77	.367	-2.8	2B(34): -2.1, CF(30): -0.0, 3B(10): -0.9	-0.4
2020	DET	MLB	26	54	97	.447	0.1	LF(6): 0.0, 3B(4): 0.1, RF(4): 0.3	0.1
2021 FS	DET	MLB	27	600	75	.323	0.4	3B 1, RF 0	-0.3
2021 DC	DET	MLB	27	271	75	.323	0.2	3B 0, RF 0	-0.3

Kody Clemens 2B

Born: 05/15/96 Age: 25 Bats: L Throws: R
Height: 6'1" Weight: 170 Origin: Round 3, 2018 Draft (#79 overall)

YEAR	TEAM	LVL	AGE	PA	R	2B	3B	HR	RBI	BB	K	SB	CS	AVG/OBP/SLG
2018	WM	LO-A	22	174	18	10	2	4	17	21	27	3	1	.302/.387/.477
2018	LAK	HI-A	22	46	6	2	0	1	3	2	12	1	0	.238/.283/.357
2019	LAK	HI-A	23	469	43	24	7	11	59	45	101	11	3	.238/.314/.411
2019	ERI	AA	23	54	5	2	0	1	4	6	18	0	0	.170/.278/.277
2021 FS	DET	MLB	25	600	57	24	4	16	64	42	173	2	2	.218/.280/.370

Comparables: Ryan Schimpf, Taylor Featherston, Sam Haggerty

Famous-named second baseman Clemens spent last summer on a makeshift independent league team managed by his dad and oldest brother. He is the youngest of Roger's four large adult sons and has the best chance of any of them to become a big leaguer. One of the Constellation Energy League's ballclubs, the Sugar Land Skeeters, got promoted to Triple-A as the Astros' affiliate; Clemens can only hope to follow suit.

YEAR	TEAM	LVL	AGE	PA	DRC+	BABIP	BRR	FRAA	WARP
2018	WM	LO-A	22	174	140	.342	-0.9	2B(39): -1.6	0.8
2018	LAK	HI-A	22	46	66	.300	0.3	2B(11): 0.2	-0.1
2019	LAK	HI-A	23	469	112	.283	-2.3	2B(99): -0.7	1.4
2019	ERI	AA	23	54	54	.250	-0.6	2B(13): 1.6	0.0
2021 FS	DET	MLB	25	600	76	.286	0.0	2B 0	0.0

Dillon Dingler C

Born: 09/17/98 Age: 22 Bats: R Throws: R
Height: 6'3" Weight: 210 Origin: Round 2, 2020 Draft (#38 overall)

Dingler's truncated junior season had 10 extra-base hits in 13 games (half of 'em homers) with legitimate catching defense that put the scouts on notice, giving him sudden first-round potential, but second-round reality. Still, he John Hancocked a record signing bonus for an Ohio State Buckeye, surpassing Nick Swisher 18 years prior, though he likely won't get his own chapter in a Michael Lewis book about it. He spent some time in the Tigers' 60-man pool, but being relatively new at catching (he was a center fielder two years ago), we likely won't see him swishing or dingling in the majors for at least a few years.

Detroit Tigers 2021

Greg Garcia 2B
Born: 08/08/89   Age: 31   Bats: L   Throws: R
Height: 6'0"   Weight: 200   Origin: Round 7, 2010 Draft (#229 overall)

YEAR	TEAM	LVL	AGE	PA	R	2B	3B	HR	RBI	BB	K	SB	CS	AVG/OBP/SLG
2018	STL	MLB	28	208	15	6	0	3	15	20	37	3	1	.221/.309/.304
2019	SD	MLB	29	372	52	13	4	4	31	53	83	0	2	.248/.364/.354
2020	SD	MLB	30	71	6	3	0	0	11	7	18	1	0	.200/.279/.250
2021 FS	DET	MLB	31	600	59	20	2	9	54	74	143	3	3	.226/.335/.331

Comparables: Dave Berg, Damian Jackson, Frank Menechino

When your only offensive skill is being able to take a walk...well, sooner or later you're going to be told to take a walk. Garcia, who barely hit last year and is on the wrong side of 30, is nearing that point.

YEAR	TEAM	LVL	AGE	PA	DRC+	BABIP	BRR	FRAA	WARP
2018	STL	MLB	28	208	80	.259	0.2	2B(31): -0.4, SS(17): 1.9, 3B(15): -0.5	0.4
2019	SD	MLB	29	372	87	.323	2.4	2B(74): 2.1, 3B(13): -0.6, SS(9): 0.2	1.1
2020	SD	MLB	30	71	73	.279	1.0	2B(11): 0.4, 3B(10): 0.6	0.2
2021 FS	DET	MLB	31	600	88	.295	-0.3	2B 0, 3B 0	0.9

Dustin Garneau C
Born: 08/13/87   Age: 33   Bats: R   Throws: R
Height: 6'2"   Weight: 205   Origin: Round 19, 2009 Draft (#571 overall)

YEAR	TEAM	LVL	AGE	PA	R	2B	3B	HR	RBI	BB	K	SB	CS	AVG/OBP/SLG
2018	CHA	AAA	30	160	19	9	0	7	22	16	38	0	2	.252/.340/.468
2018	NAS	AAA	30	80	8	3	0	2	9	5	10	0	0	.208/.263/.333
2018	CHW	MLB	30	3	0	0	0	0	1	1	0	0	0	.500/.667/.500
2019	SL	AAA	31	98	16	8	0	6	13	11	28	0	0	.229/.347/.542
2019	LV	AAA	31	32	2	2	1	1	3	3	9	0	0	.308/.387/.577
2019	LAA	MLB	31	82	11	3	0	2	7	8	17	0	0	.232/.346/.362
2019	OAK	MLB	31	19	3	2	0	1	7	2	4	0	0	.294/.368/.588
2020	HOU	MLB	32	46	4	0	1	1	4	6	15	0	0	.158/.273/.289
2021 FS	DET	MLB	33	600	65	19	1	24	72	52	173	0	1	.201/.286/.377

Comparables: Jose Lobaton, Josh Phegley, Dusty Wathan

The out-of-options Garneau discovered that being the primary backup has its disadvantages compared to the third catcher role. He has never started more than 33 big-league games in a season or caught over 300 innings at the level. Garneau would get his reps by catching several hundred more innings at Triple-A, a level where he'd also been excellent with the stick. Playing behind Martín Maldonado provided little more work than backing up Yadier Molina: Garneau was lucky if he saw more than a handful of plate appearances a week and caught barely 20 percent of the team's innings, going as many as nine games between starts. Extra rest did not seem to help his performance. His final start for the team took that to a new extreme, coming in ALCS Game 3, 16 days after his final regular season start. He struck out in both plate appearances. If Garneau just wants to play, the Astros waiving him might not be the worst thing in the world.

YEAR	TEAM	P. COUNT	FRM RUNS	BLK RUNS	THRW RUNS	TOT RUNS
2018	CHW	154	0.0	0.1	0.0	0.1
2018	NAS	2512	-2.1	-0.2	0.7	-1.6
2019	OAK	703	0.1	-0.2	0.0	-0.1
2019	LAA	3375	0.4	0.0	0.0	0.4
2019	SL	3857	7.2	0.1	0.6	7.9
2020	HOU	1966	-0.1	-0.3	0.1	-0.3
2021	DET	16650	-9.4	-1.5	-0.4	-11.3
2021	DET	16650	-9.4	-2.1	-0.4	-11.9

YEAR	TEAM	LVL	AGE	PA	DRC+	BABIP	BRR	FRAA	WARP
2018	CHA	AAA	30	160	113	.295	-0.3	C(39): -0.9, 1B(1): -0.3, LF(1): -0.2	0.5
2018	NAS	AAA	30	80	67	.210	-1.3	C(18): -2.2	-0.4
2018	CHW	MLB	30	3	98	.500	0.0	C(1): -0.3	0.0
2019	SL	AAA	31	98	91	.265	-0.6	C(26): 8.7	1.1
2019	LV	AAA	31	32	99	.412	-1.0	C(7): -0.1, 1B(1): 0.0	0.1
2019	LAA	MLB	31	82	87	.280	-0.5	C(27): -0.0, 1B(1): -0.0	0.2
2019	OAK	MLB	31	19	108	.333	-0.2	C(7): -0.0	0.1
2020	HOU	MLB	32	46	70	.227	0.0	C(17): -0.2	-0.1
2021 FS	DET	MLB	33	600	77	.250	-0.7	C -13, 1B 0	-0.7

Detroit Tigers 2021

Riley Greene   RF
Born: 09/28/00   Age: 20   Bats: L   Throws: L
Height: 6'3"   Weight: 200   Origin: Round 1, 2019 Draft (#5 overall)

YEAR	TEAM	LVL	AGE	PA	R	2B	3B	HR	RBI	BB	K	SB	CS	AVG/OBP/SLG
2019	TIW	ROK	18	43	9	3	0	2	8	5	12	0	0	.351/.442/.595
2019	NOR	SS	18	100	12	3	1	1	7	11	25	1	0	.295/.380/.386
2019	WM	LO-A	18	108	13	2	2	2	13	6	26	4	0	.219/.278/.344
2021 FS	DET	MLB	20	600	47	21	4	9	52	34	209	5	2	.200/.253/.306

Comparables: Luis Alexander Basabe, Harold Ramirez, Manuel Margot

It's July in Comerica Park, and Greene just robbed someone of a home run by reaching over the left field wall. This may be a lucid dream about the future of the team but it was literally last year's training camp, and a reminder that there's a very exciting outfielder waiting in the wings. The 20-year-old with baseball-smacking potential probably would have completed his High-A season in The Normal Times, so this year's league will presumably contain multiple vowels.

YEAR	TEAM	LVL	AGE	PA	DRC+	BABIP	BRR	FRAA	WARP
2019	TIW	ROK	18	43		.478			
2019	NOR	SS	18	100	127	.403	-1.5	CF(21): 3.5	0.7
2019	WM	LO-A	18	108	62	.268	0.8	CF(20): 1.9, RF(4): -0.0	0.2
2021 FS	DET	MLB	20	600	53	.300	0.4	CF 9, RF 1	-0.8

Grayson Greiner   C
Born: 10/11/92   Age: 28   Bats: R   Throws: R
Height: 6'6"   Weight: 239   Origin: Round 3, 2014 Draft (#99 overall)

YEAR	TEAM	LVL	AGE	PA	R	2B	3B	HR	RBI	BB	K	SB	CS	AVG/OBP/SLG
2018	TOL	AAA	25	180	12	8	1	4	23	21	42	0	0	.266/.350/.405
2018	DET	MLB	25	116	9	6	0	0	12	17	32	0	1	.219/.328/.281
2019	TOL	AAA	26	53	8	1	0	2	4	4	16	0	0	.250/.321/.396
2019	DET	MLB	26	224	18	5	1	5	19	13	70	0	0	.202/.251/.308
2020	DET	MLB	27	55	8	2	0	3	8	3	20	0	0	.118/.182/.333
2021 FS	DET	MLB	28	600	61	22	3	16	60	48	196	0	1	.206/.276/.349
2021 DC	DET	MLB	28	213	21	7	1	5	21	17	69	0	0	.206/.276/.349

Comparables: Ron Karkovice, Paul Bako, Jeff Mathis

"Missing: tall catcher." Greiner's whereabouts are completely known, but this poster is a complete scouting summary of his hitting, size and primary position.

YEAR	TEAM	P. COUNT	FRM RUNS	BLK RUNS	THRW RUNS	TOT RUNS
2018	DET	4496	-0.6	-0.2	0.0	-0.9
2018	TOL	6038	9.5	0.5	0.3	10.3
2019	DET	8636	-2.4	0.3	0.2	-2.0
2019	TOL	1168	1.2	0.0	0.0	1.2
2020	DET	2451	-0.3	0.0	0.0	-0.3
2021	*DET*	*8418*	*-1.5*	*-0.6*	*-0.1*	*-2.1*
2021	*DET*	*8418*	*-1.5*	*-0.7*	*-0.1*	*-2.3*

YEAR	TEAM	LVL	AGE	PA	DRC+	BABIP	BRR	FRAA	WARP
2018	TOL	AAA	25	180	115	.336	0.3	C(44): 11.2	2.1
2018	DET	MLB	25	116	78	.313	0.3	C(30): -0.5	0.3
2019	TOL	AAA	26	53	89	.333	0.5	C(9): 1.1	0.3
2019	DET	MLB	26	224	55	.276	-0.9	C(58): -2.9	-0.5
2020	DET	MLB	27	55	78	.107	-0.3	C(18): -0.3	-0.1
2021 FS	*DET*	*MLB*	*28*	*600*	*73*	*.288*	*-0.5*	*C -4*	*-0.1*
2021 DC	*DET*	*MLB*	*28*	*213*	*73*	*.288*	*-0.2*	*C -2*	*-0.1*

Robbie Grossman LF
Born: 09/16/89 Age: 31 Bats: S Throws: L
Height: 6'0" Weight: 216 Origin: Round 6, 2008 Draft (#174 overall)

YEAR	TEAM	LVL	AGE	PA	R	2B	3B	HR	RBI	BB	K	SB	CS	AVG/OBP/SLG
2018	MIN	MLB	28	465	50	27	1	5	48	60	83	0	1	.273/.367/.384
2019	OAK	MLB	29	482	57	21	3	6	38	59	86	9	4	.240/.334/.348
2020	OAK	MLB	30	192	23	12	2	8	23	21	38	8	1	.241/.344/.482
2021 FS	*DET*	*MLB*	*31*	*600*	*64*	*24*	*2*	*13*	*57*	*77*	*134*	*4*	*3*	*.233/.338/.369*
2021 DC	*DET*	*MLB*	*31*	*525*	*56*	*21*	*1*	*11*	*50*	*67*	*117*	*4*	*2*	*.233/.338/.369*

Comparables: Jack Voigt, Daniel Nava, Jason Michaels

Mathematically, a gross refers to a dozen dozen, 144, of something. It's etymologically distinct from the other definitions of gross, and the term's use is encouraged by the Dozenal Society of America (which advocates for a base-12 numerical system). By that metric, Grossman's 2020 season was as unsuccessful as each of his major league seasons, and all campaigns since his 144 DRC+ in Triple-A in 2014. By most other metrics, it was a career year for the 31-year-old, who was above average at the plate, in the field, *and* on the basepaths for a three-win pace thanks to a new pull-heavy, fly ball approach. The DRC+ likely won't ever reach gross heights, though his 119 mark was just short of a great gross (120) and looks to be repeatable.

Detroit Tigers 2021

YEAR	TEAM	LVL	AGE	PA	DRC+	BABIP	BRR	FRAA	WARP
2018	MIN	MLB	28	465	105	.329	-4.9	RF(52): -2.6, LF(34): 1.2	0.6
2019	OAK	MLB	29	482	96	.288	-4.3	LF(112): 3.2, RF(20): -1.3, CF(1): 0.1	0.9
2020	OAK	MLB	30	192	119	.267	0.9	LF(46): 2.7, CF(2): 0.0, RF(1): -0.1	1.1
2021 FS	*DET*	*MLB*	*31*	*600*	*100*	*.289*	*-0.3*	*LF 3, RF 0*	*1.7*
2021 DC	*DET*	*MLB*	*31*	*525*	*100*	*.289*	*-0.3*	*LF 2, RF 0*	*1.5*

Derek Hill CF
Born: 12/30/95   Age: 25   Bats: R   Throws: R
Height: 6'2"   Weight: 190   Origin: Round 1, 2014 Draft (#23 overall)

YEAR	TEAM	LVL	AGE	PA	R	2B	3B	HR	RBI	BB	K	SB	CS	AVG/OBP/SLG
2018	LAK	HI-A	22	383	45	9	3	4	33	33	109	35	12	.239/.307/.318
2019	ERI	AA	23	526	78	19	5	14	45	38	147	21	13	.243/.311/.394
2020	DET	MLB	24	12	3	0	0	0	1	6	0	0	.091/.167/.091
2021 FS	*DET*	*MLB*	*25*	*600*	*52*	*24*	*6*	*11*	*58*	*42*	*213*	*23*	*9*	*.214/.277/.348*

Comparables: Matthew den Dekker, Xavier Avery, Daniel Fields

Once a highly regarded prospect, Hill's development was interrupted by nagging injuries, but thanks to someone else's fractured hand, he finally hit the big leagues six years after his first-round christening. He can run, field and throw, and he's got a real knack for highlight-reel diving catches. Assuming this is the complete list of skills one needs as a position player, he's good as gold.

YEAR	TEAM	LVL	AGE	PA	DRC+	BABIP	BRR	FRAA	WARP
2018	LAK	HI-A	22	383	82	.338	3.7	CF(55): -2.5, LF(27): -2.1, RF(21): 0.4	-0.5
2019	ERI	AA	23	526	92	.321	0.7	CF(80): 1.4, RF(37): 7.8, LF(2): -0.2	2.2
2020	DET	MLB	24	12	67	.200	0.0	CF(10): -0.2	-0.1
2021 FS	*DET*	*MLB*	*25*	*600*	*71*	*.325*	*2.9*	*CF 2, RF 5*	*0.4*

Parker Meadows   CF
Born: 11/02/99   Age: 21   Bats: L   Throws: R
Height: 6'5"   Weight: 205   Origin: Round 2, 2018 Draft (#44 overall)

YEAR	TEAM	LVL	AGE	PA	R	2B	3B	HR	RBI	BB	K	SB	CS	AVG/OBP/SLG
2018	TIW	ROK	18	85	16	2	1	4	8	8	25	3	1	.284/.376/.500
2018	NOR	SS	18	21	4	1	0	0	2	2	6	0	0	.316/.381/.368
2019	WM	LO-A	19	504	52	15	2	7	40	47	113	14	8	.221/.296/.312
2021 FS	*DET*	*MLB*	*21*	*600*	*46*	*21*	*3*	*9*	*51*	*36*	*205*	*7*	*4*	*.196/.249/.298*

Comparables: Derrick Robinson, Mickey Moniak, Carlos Tocci

Meadows spent the summer at the Tigers' alternate site, with the aim of making mechanical adjustments to a long swing that contributed to his struggles in his first stint in full-season ball. Until he makes some movement in the minors, he'll henceforth be known as Austin's little brother, not to be confused with the other Austin's little brother: Round Rock.

YEAR	TEAM	LVL	AGE	PA	DRC+	BABIP	BRR	FRAA	WARP
2018	TIW	ROK	18	85		.378			
2018	NOR	SS	18	21	97	.462	0.1	CF(6): 0.0	0.0
2019	WM	LO-A	19	504	78	.277	-1.1	CF(101): -2.3, RF(16): 0.8	0.0
2021 FS	*DET*	*MLB*	*21*	*600*	*48*	*.289*	*0.5*	*CF 5, RF 1*	*-1.5*

Jake Rogers C

Born: 04/18/95   Age: 26   Bats: R   Throws: R
Height: 6'1"   Weight: 192   Origin: Round 3, 2016 Draft (#97 overall)

YEAR	TEAM	LVL	AGE	PA	R	2B	3B	HR	RBI	BB	K	SB	CS	AVG/OBP/SLG
2018	ERI	AA	23	408	57	15	1	17	56	41	112	7	1	.219/.305/.412
2019	ERI	AA	24	112	17	3	1	5	21	19	26	0	0	.302/.429/.535
2019	TOL	AAA	24	191	29	10	1	9	31	18	53	0	0	.223/.321/.458
2019	DET	MLB	24	128	11	3	0	4	8	13	51	0	0	.125/.222/.259
2021 FS	DET	MLB	26	600	61	18	4	19	62	53	204	2	2	.194/.278/.352
2021 DC	DET	MLB	26	61	6	1	0	1	6	5	20	0	0	.194/.278/.352

Comparables: Lucas May, Luke Montz, Tom Murphy

The defensively pragmatic Rogers took a year off from collecting major league stats against his will, though putting a year's worth of natural calamity between himself and his 2019 production couldn't hurt his standing. Whether or not he remains the Tigers' catcher of the future, and whether or not this is levied as a criticism toward said future, Rogers should be able to bang just enough bombs to justify a catcher's batting average equal to your average league bowling score.

YEAR	TEAM	P. COUNT	FRM RUNS	BLK RUNS	THRW RUNS	TOT RUNS
2019	DET	5389	-1.4	-2.2	0.2	-3.3
2019	TOL	6997	7.3	0.0	1.2	8.4
2021	DET	2405	0.0	-0.9	-0.1	-1.0
2021	DET	2405	0.0	-1.0	-0.1	-1.1

YEAR	TEAM	LVL	AGE	PA	DRC+	BABIP	BRR	FRAA	WARP
2018	ERI	AA	23	408	88	.261	2.7	C(98): 29.4, 1B(1): 0.0	4.2
2019	ERI	AA	24	112	164	.356	-1.7	C(21): 2.3	1.2
2019	TOL	AAA	24	191	88	.269	-2.7	C(48): 9.5	1.3
2019	DET	MLB	24	128	52	.175	-0.4	C(34): -4.0	-0.6
2021 FS	DET	MLB	26	600	76	.269	0.1	C -7, 1B 0	-0.1
2021 DC	DET	MLB	26	61	76	.269	0.0	C -1	0.0

Christin Stewart LF

Born: 12/10/93   Age: 27   Bats: L   Throws: R
Height: 6'0"   Weight: 220   Origin: Round 1, 2015 Draft (#34 overall)

YEAR	TEAM	LVL	AGE	PA	R	2B	3B	HR	RBI	BB	K	SB	CS	AVG/OBP/SLG
2018	TOL	AAA	24	522	69	21	3	23	77	67	108	0	0	.264/.364/.480
2018	DET	MLB	24	72	7	1	1	2	10	10	13	0	0	.267/.375/.417
2019	LAK	HI-A	25	25	2	1	0	1	5	3	3	0	0	.350/.400/.550
2019	TOL	AAA	25	102	14	2	0	4	14	18	25	1	0	.289/.422/.458
2019	DET	MLB	25	416	32	25	1	10	40	34	103	0	1	.233/.305/.388
2020	DET	MLB	26	99	6	3	0	3	9	5	30	0	0	.167/.224/.300
2021 FS	DET	MLB	27	600	66	24	3	22	70	56	177	0	0	.216/.304/.401
2021 DC	DET	MLB	27	100	11	4	0	3	11	9	29	0	0	.216/.304/.401

Comparables: Larry Bigbie, Alex Gordon, Ryan Langerhans

One way to define potential energy is to picture a rock at the top of a hill. It has the potential to roll down and collide into something. The higher the hill, the more potential energy the rock possesses. Stewart is that rock on a hill and has yet to budge. This is because he's having trouble hitting anything other than a fastball, which certainly won't play well in a highly televised professional league. He has a long track record of beltin' from the left side in the minors, but with lumbering instincts in the outfield, he'll need to start hitting like a DH (designated hitter) or else become DH (dormant on a hill).

YEAR	TEAM	LVL	AGE	PA	DRC+	BABIP	BRR	FRAA	WARP
2018	TOL	AAA	24	522	136	.296	0.8	LF(97): 9.8, RF(12): -0.7	3.5
2018	DET	MLB	24	72	106	.304	-0.3	LF(15): -0.9	0.1
2019	LAK	HI-A	25	25	144	.333	0.2	LF(3): -0.4	0.1
2019	TOL	AAA	25	102	139	.370	-0.1	LF(16): -3.4	0.4
2019	DET	MLB	25	416	85	.290	-4.1	LF(89): -12.5	-1.3
2020	DET	MLB	26	99	75	.207	-0.1	LF(32): -1.0	-0.3
2021 FS	DET	MLB	27	600	93	.278	-0.5	LF 0, RF 0	0.9
2021 DC	DET	MLB	27	100	93	.278	-0.1	LF 0	0.1

Detroit Tigers 2021

Spencer Torkelson   3B
Born: 08/26/99   Age: 21   Bats: R   Throws: R
Height: 6'1"   Weight: 220   Origin: Round 1, 2020 Draft (#1 overall)

A 70-grade name if you're a mechanical engineer, Torkelson and his power bat should've replaced Adrián González at the turn of the century as the most recent first baseman to be yoinked first by a bunch of performative dorks in the MLB Draft. But Detroit has a premonition of trying him out at third base (since that worked out so well for Miguel Cabrera for about three minutes), instead making this factoid about Phil Nevin in 1992. The young man spent last year splashing around in the 60-man player pool, working with Hall of Fame luminaries such as Alan Trammell, a man whom Torkelson sheepishly admitted he had not heard of until being drafted. He broke a Barry Bonds home run school record at Arizona State as a freshman, and once he gets to the major leagues, he almost certainly will not do that again.

Jake Brigham   RHP
Born: 02/10/88   Age: 33   Bats: R   Throws: R
Height: 6'3"   Weight: 210   Origin: Round 6, 2006 Draft (#178 overall)

YEAR	TEAM	LVL	AGE	W	L	SV	G	GS	IP	H	HR	BB/9	K/9	K	GB%	BABIP
2018	KIW	KBO	30	11	7	0	31	30	199	188	19	2.0	7.9	175		
2019	KIW	KBO	31	13	5	0	28	28	158^1	148	5	2.0	7.4	130		
2020	KIW	KBO	32	9	5	0	21	21	107	98	6	3.0	8.8	105		
2021									No projection							

In the KBO, where teams may only sign three non-Korean players, it's vital to use those roster spaces wisely. That applies double for contenders in a season like last year where the difference between fifth place (and two do-or-die games to advance) and second place (a bye until the semifinals) amounted to a single game in the standings. That brings us to Brigham, who has headlined Kiwoom's rotation for four years now. The former Atlanta Brave once again turned in a solid season, notching a 131 ERA+ while striking out nearly a batter per inning. Unfortunately, what he provided in quality he lacked in volume. Brigham strained his elbow in his first outing, and ultimately missed 10 starts. Oftentimes, such an injury will prompt KBO clubs to seek a replacement, as the penalty for replacing a former major leaguer with a long reliever in the rotation is very stiff in this league. But, given the pandemic and perhaps the equity Brigham had built up, the Heroes decided to keep him on the roster. All those missed starts added up in the end, as Kiwoom found themselves in the dreaded fifth slot for the playoffs. Sometimes, loyalty isn't cheap.

YEAR	TEAM	LVL	AGE	WHIP	ERA	DRA-	WARP	MPH	FB%	WHF	CSP
2018	KIW	KBO	30	1.20	3.84						
2019	KIW	KBO	31	1.23	2.96						
2020	KIW	KBO	32	1.31	3.62						
2021						No projection					

Beau Burrows   RHP
Born: 09/18/96   Age: 24   Bats: R   Throws: R
Height: 6'2"   Weight: 210   Origin: Round 1, 2015 Draft (#22 overall)

YEAR	TEAM	LVL	AGE	W	L	SV	G	GS	IP	H	HR	BB/9	K/9	K	GB%	BABIP
2018	ERI	AA	21	10	9	0	26	26	134	126	12	3.8	8.5	127	30.3%	.311
2019	TOL	AAA	22	2	6	0	15	15	65¹	68	12	4.4	8.4	61	34.5%	.303
2020	DET	MLB	23	0	0	0	5	0	6²	8	3	1.4	4.0	3	40.0%	.227
2021 FS	DET	MLB	24	2	3	0	57	0	50	50	8	4.3	7.8	43	34.4%	.292
2021 DC	DET	MLB	24	3	2	0	28	3	33	33	5	4.3	7.8	28	34.4%	.292

Comparables: Nick Neidert, Luis Ortiz, Ariel Jurado

Last summer, Bo Bichette was often the target of a cascade of puns, because he's already a productive player in the major leagues and Bo rhymes with many words. And thanks to breakthrough advancements in homophone technology, Burrows could encounter the same fate now that he has finally tasted the major leagues. His fastball is low-to-mid 90s, his emerging changeup bailed him out and he's going to be well suited to round out the rotation this year. Threau Burrows.

YEAR	TEAM	LVL	AGE	WHIP	ERA	DRA-	WARP	MPH	FB%	WHF	CSP
2018	ERI	AA	21	1.36	4.10	148	-2.6				
2019	TOL	AAA	22	1.53	5.51	117	0.6				
2020	DET	MLB	23	1.35	5.40	122	0.0	95.1	54.5%	19.6%	
2021 FS	DET	MLB	24	1.49	5.25	116	-0.2	95.1	54.5%	19.6%	47.1%
2021 DC	DET	MLB	24	1.49	5.25	116	-0.1	95.1	54.5%	19.6%	47.1%

Ryan Carpenter   LHP
Born: 08/22/90   Age: 30   Bats: L   Throws: L
Height: 6'5"   Weight: 230   Origin: Round 7, 2011 Draft (#240 overall)

YEAR	TEAM	LVL	AGE	W	L	SV	G	GS	IP	H	HR	BB/9	K/9	K	GB%	BABIP
2018	TOL	AAA	27	2	8	0	14	14	76¹	96	8	2.5	8.6	73	32.7%	.374
2018	DET	MLB	27	1	2	0	6	5	22¹	34	8	1.6	6.0	15	34.1%	.338
2019	TOL	AAA	28	5	7	0	14	14	77	77	11	3.0	8.9	76	41.5%	.310
2019	DET	MLB	28	1	6	0	9	9	40²	61	12	2.9	5.5	25	36.3%	.338
2020	RAK	CPBL	29	11	7	0	29	28	172²	194	14	1.8	8.9	170		
2021 FS	DET	MLB	30	2	3	0	57	0	50	54	10	2.9	7.6	42	37.1%	.299

Comparables: Jerad Eickhoff, Matt Koch, Justin Haley

Detroit Tigers 2021

Even when they were the class of the league in the first month or two of the season, the Monkeys were never exactly known for their pitching. That being said, Carpenter added some stability to the Rakuten staff, leading their starters in ERA and strikeouts while effectively limiting walks and homers. The long-time Tigers farmhand appeared for some brief, unmemorable stints with the big league team in 2018 and 2019. But his solid work in 2020 reportedly turned some heads, as there were rumors in August that a KBO team was looking to lure Carpenter away from the Monkeys for their stretch run. That ticket finally arrived in the offseason; he'll move up—and down—to the KBO, and to its worst team, the Hanwha Eagles, in 2021.

YEAR	TEAM	LVL	AGE	WHIP	ERA	DRA-	WARP	MPH	FB%	WHF	CSP
2018	TOL	AAA	27	1.53	5.07	93	0.8				
2018	DET	MLB	27	1.70	7.25	129	-0.1	91.7	51.6%	20.9%	
2019	TOL	AAA	28	1.34	5.26	97	1.5				
2019	DET	MLB	28	1.82	9.30	185	-1.4	91.9	45.2%	16.2%	
2020	RAK	CPBL	29	1.33	3.81						
2021 FS	*DET*	*MLB*	*30*	*1.41*	*5.37*	*119*	*-0.3*	*91.8*	*46.8%*	*17.3%*	*51.7%*

Alex Faedo RHP
Born: 11/12/95 Age: 25 Bats: R Throws: R
Height: 6'5" Weight: 225 Origin: Round 1, 2017 Draft (#18 overall)

YEAR	TEAM	LVL	AGE	W	L	SV	G	GS	IP	H	HR	BB/9	K/9	K	GB%	BABIP
2018	LAK	HI-A	22	2	4	0	12	12	61	49	3	1.9	7.5	51	32.0%	.263
2018	ERI	AA	22	3	6	0	12	12	60	54	15	3.3	8.8	59	26.3%	.250
2019	ERI	AA	23	6	7	0	22	22	115[1]	104	17	2.0	10.5	134	32.5%	.299
2021 FS	*DET*	*MLB*	*25*	*2*	*3*	*0*	*57*	*0*	*50*	*47*	*8*	*3.2*	*8.7*	*48*	*31.5%*	*.288*

Comparables: Jordan Yamamoto, Ryan Helsley, Robert Dugger

Injuries and COVID-19 quarantine caused Faedo to miss time throwing in nebulous stat-free environments. The former first-rounder and College World Series hero will be in the majors soon, however, ready to disappoint the fans in attendance who thought they might get to see Mize or Manning. Not that there's anything wrong with Faedo; he's developed into a perfectly adequate back-end starter, with a fastball that technically reaches the plate and a slider that can miss enough bats to get him out of the inning after five or so batters. There are worse things, and folks in Detroit have been watching them for a few years, so fan expectations will find a suitable baseline in Faedo, in all his high-floor, low-ceiling glory.

YEAR	TEAM	LVL	AGE	WHIP	ERA	DRA-	WARP	MPH	FB%	WHF	CSP
2018	LAK	HI-A	22	1.02	3.10	66	1.5				
2018	ERI	AA	22	1.27	4.95	94	0.6				
2019	ERI	AA	23	1.12	3.90	77	1.7				
2021 FS	DET	MLB	25	1.32	4.41	105	0.1				

Matt Manning   RHP

Born: 01/28/98   Age: 23   Bats: R   Throws: R
Height: 6'6"   Weight: 195   Origin: Round 1, 2016 Draft (#9 overall)

YEAR	TEAM	LVL	AGE	W	L	SV	G	GS	IP	H	HR	BB/9	K/9	K	GB%	BABIP
2018	WM	LO-A	20	3	3	0	11	11	55^2	47	3	4.5	12.3	76	40.5%	.346
2018	LAK	HI-A	20	4	4	0	9	9	51^1	32	4	3.3	11.4	65	45.8%	.243
2018	ERI	AA	20	0	1	0	2	2	10^2	11	0	3.4	11.0	13	39.3%	.423
2019	ERI	AA	21	11	5	0	24	24	133^2	93	7	2.6	10.0	148	47.2%	.259
2021 FS	DET	MLB	23	9	8	0	26	26	150	126	18	4.4	9.5	157	43.5%	.278
2021 DC	DET	MLB	23	3	3	0	12	11	55.3	46	7	4.4	9.5	58	43.5%	.278

Comparables: Luis Severino, Ian Anderson, Stephen Gonsalves

Six Tigers prospects made their major league debuts in 2020. Manning wasn't one of them, having suffered the same type of forearm strain that befell Alex Faedo. Things looked grim, especially under the cloaking device that is the alternate training site, but the fears seem to be unfounded; he declared that in a normal season, the injury would have shut him down for a few weeks at most. That puts him in line to be ready for 2021, if 2021 itself is, and to co-chair a rotation with Casey Mize that will prove one of the most exciting of the young decade. A two-sport prep talent who remodeled his delivery in the minors, Manning's arsenal is still a little less refined than his collegiate colleagues, but his ceiling is as high as anyone's, and it'll be fun to watch him reach for it.

YEAR	TEAM	LVL	AGE	WHIP	ERA	DRA-	WARP	MPH	FB%	WHF	CSP
2018	WM	LO-A	20	1.35	3.40	69	1.3				
2018	LAK	HI-A	20	0.99	2.98	76	1.0				
2018	ERI	AA	20	1.41	4.22	65	0.3				
2019	ERI	AA	21	0.98	2.56	56	3.6				
2021 FS	DET	MLB	23	1.34	3.91	93	2.0				
2021 DC	DET	MLB	23	1.34	3.91	93	0.8				

Detroit Tigers 2021

Franklin Pérez   RHP
Born: 12/06/97   Age: 23   Bats: R   Throws: R
Height: 6'3"   Weight: 197   Origin: International Free Agent, 2014

YEAR	TEAM	LVL	AGE	W	L	SV	G	GS	IP	H	HR	BB/9	K/9	K	GB%	BABIP
2018	TIG	ROK	20	0	1	0	3	3	8	3	0	0.0	5.6	5	27.3%	.136
2018	LAK	HI-A	20	0	1	0	4	4	11^1	15	2	6.4	7.1	9	43.2%	.371
2019	LAK	HI-A	21	0	0	0	2	2	7^2	7	1	5.9	7.0	6	45.5%	.286
2021 FS	DET	MLB	23	2	2	0	57	0	50	47	6	4.0	7.5	41	33.9%	.283

Comparables: Michael Fulmer, Junior Fernández, Duane Underwood Jr.

It's no small irony that Pérez was finally healthy the season there was no season. It's hard to even conceptualize a full year from the young righty, who has pitched just 27 professional innings since being the marquee prospect in the Justin Verlander trade; the future Hall-of-Famer matched that workload in the 2017 postseason alone. Pérez is still just 22 but has a mountain of memories to make up. It's another irony that because of the injuries, and his spot on the 40-man roster dictated by his (inactive) service time, he wasn't able to attend some much-needed instructional league work with the other prospects his age. Instead, the Tigers will hope their time with him at the alternate site did some good, and that he'll start next season at Double-A.

YEAR	TEAM	LVL	AGE	WHIP	ERA	DRA-	WARP	MPH	FB%	WHF	CSP
2018	TIG	ROK	20	0.38	4.50						
2018	LAK	HI-A	20	2.03	7.94	111	0.0				
2019	LAK	HI-A	21	1.57	2.35	126	-0.1				
2021 FS	DET	MLB	23	1.41	4.47	103	0.1				

Joey Wentz LHP
Born: 10/06/97   Age: 23   Bats: L   Throws: L
Height: 6'5"   Weight: 220   Origin: Round 1, 2016 Draft (#40 overall)

YEAR	TEAM	LVL	AGE	W	L	SV	G	GS	IP	H	HR	BB/9	K/9	K	GB%	BABIP
2018	DAY	HI-A	20	0	0	0	1	1	4	1	0	2.2	4.5	2		.091
2018	FLO	HI-A	20	3	4	0	16	16	67	49	3	3.2	7.1	53	44.4%	.251
2019	MIS	AA	21	5	8	0	20	20	103	90	13	3.9	8.7	100	32.6%	.283
2019	ERI	AA	21	2	0	0	5	5	25^2	20	3	1.4	13.0	37	19.3%	.315
2021 FS	DET	MLB	23	2	3	0	57	0	50	47	8	4.9	8.6	48	32.3%	.287

Comparables: Trevor Rogers, Génesis Cabrera, Lucas Giolito

Wentz, the next-in-line Tigers pitching prospect, took the Tommy John pledge last March; he should be ready to heave the ol' pellet in the general direction of uniformed athletes by midsummer. He lacks the pure stuff of the Mizes and Mannings who went before him, and is more likely to prove a fourth starter than a second, but he does wield a nasty, fading changeup that serves as an out pitch. The goal will be for him to see the majors by September.

YEAR	TEAM	LVL	AGE	WHIP	ERA	DRA-	WARP	MPH	FB%	WHF	CSP
2018	DAY	HI-A	20	0.50	0.00						
2018	FLO	HI-A	20	1.09	2.28	86	0.9				
2019	MIS	AA	21	1.31	4.72	113	-0.7				
2019	ERI	AA	21	0.94	2.10	67	0.5				
2021 FS	DET	MLB	23	1.50	4.98	111	-0.1				

Jordan Zimmermann RHP

Born: 05/23/86   Age: 35   Bats: R   Throws: R
Height: 6'2"   Weight: 225   Origin: Round 2, 2007 Draft (#67 overall)

YEAR	TEAM	LVL	AGE	W	L	SV	G	GS	IP	H	HR	BB/9	K/9	K	GB%	BABIP
2018	DET	MLB	32	7	8	0	25	25	131^1	140	28	1.8	7.6	111	36.2%	.289
2019	DET	MLB	33	1	13	0	23	23	112	145	19	2.0	6.6	82	41.4%	.341
2020	DET	MLB	34	0	0	0	3	2	5^2	11	0	3.2	9.5	6	45.0%	.550
2021 FS	DET	MLB	35	2	2	0	57	0	50	52	8	2.1	7.0	38	40.2%	.291

Comparables: Johnny Cueto, Ricky Nolasco, Homer Bailey

Five years and $110 million ago, Zimmermann entered Detroit as the seemingly final piece of a team with one last chance to contend. He began the 2016 season with an 0.55 ERA in April, a practically since-unmatched page of a calendar. The next half-decade of service was a thorough garroting of the soul, be it by injury or early exit. He limped to the finish line with a one-inning, zero-run start—a thank you for trying, if you will. We'll always have 2014, a simpler time when managers got flak for pulling pitchers in the *ninth* inning of a critical postseason game. Anyway, what we're saying is Kevin Cash will never be Zimmermann's manager.

YEAR	TEAM	LVL	AGE	WHIP	ERA	DRA-	WARP	MPH	FB%	WHF	CSP
2018	DET	MLB	32	1.26	4.52	106	0.8	92.5	45.3%	20.7%	
2019	DET	MLB	33	1.52	6.91	138	-1.2	91.5	46.9%	20.4%	
2020	DET	MLB	34	2.29	7.94	83	0.1	90.7	53.7%	18.9%	
2021 FS	DET	MLB	35	1.28	4.42	104	0.1	91.8	46.7%	20.4%	47.3%

Tigers Prospects

The State of the System:
The high-end pitching talent has scuffled recently and the system is now led by two potential impact bats. You still wonder if it's enough to fill out a competitive AL Central roster heading into Year Four of the rebuild.

The Top Ten:

───── ★ ★ ★ *2021 Top 101 Prospect* **#13** ★ ★ ★ ─────

1 **Spencer Torkelson** **3B** OFP: 70 ETA: 2022, after a few weeks in the minors to "work on his defense."
Born: 08/26/99 Age: 21 Bats: R Throws: R Height: 6'1" Weight: 220
Origin: Round 1, 2020 Draft (#1 overall)

The Report: Rare is the player who is selected as a virtually ready-made product straight out of college. There may not be much left to the imagination, except for maybe where he ends up defensively. The draft card read by Rob Manfred listed Torkelson as a third baseman despite his never having appeared at the position in college. His defensive home is inconsequential—whether it's at third or first or a corner outfield spot—because the bat is what made him the first overall pick and it will carry him to the big leagues. It's an above-average hit tool thanks to a selective approach and plus-plus power to all fields. If there is a weakness offensively, it has yet to be exposed.

Development Track: All Torkelson did while at Arizona State is obliterate most of Barry Bonds' school records. He pummeled the Pac-12 every year, crushed in the Cape Cod League, and cruised on the U.S. Collegiate National Team. He can now turn the page to be tested against pro pitching (finally), after performing very well at fall instructs. How long he spends in the minors will depend on how quickly the bat forces the Tigers' hand.

Variance: Low. Defense is almost irrelevant when 30 homers annually might be the floor.

Mark Barry's Fantasy Take:
"All Torkelson did while at Arizona State is obliterate most of Barry Bonds' school records."

Lol.

I think Torkelson is very good at hitting and that will translate to the MLB. He's a no-doubt, top-10 dynasty guy for me and could be closer to five than 10.

★ ★ ★ *2021 Top 101 Prospect* **#19** ★ ★ ★

2

Riley Greene   RF   OFP: 70   ETA: Late 2022/Early 2023
Born: 09/28/00   Age: 20   Bats: L   Throws: L   Height: 6'3"   Weight: 200
Origin: Round 1, 2019 Draft (#5 overall)

The Report: Greene's profile is one of balance. He has the five-tool potential you'd expect from a prep outfielder drafted fifth overall, but he arrived in the pro ranks in 2019 with a fairly advanced offensive game for his age and experience level. He had room to fill out and add strength, but the present frame looked the part of a future major leaguer. The hit and power tools both projected as plus despite a late hand load due to his bat speed and solid approach. The physical tools showed a potential above-average outfield glove, but Greene did struggle with his routes and reads in the big Norwich outfield and his arm might be the one place on the scouting sheet you struggle to give him at least a 5. The performance might not have been immediately loud, but you didn't have to squint hard to see a future plus regular, with breakout potential past that.

Development Track: About that breakout potential: We are about as confident as we can be for a prospect with uh … zero 2020 games played that a breakout of some sort happened. Greene added the good weight and the game power seems to be catching up to the raw. More reps in the outfield at the alternate site and instructs have smoothed out the defensive game and he's maintained most of his straight line speed for now, although I'd expect continued physical maturation in his 20s to make him a better fit in left than center. The bat will play there.

Variance: High. He did have zero real 2020 games. So we're hedging some until he's showing the same tools/skills gains in the upper minors. There was at least some discussion about whether he should rank over Torkelson though, if you want to talk about positive variance.

Mark Barry's Fantasy Take: There's no doubt that Torkelson is the No. 1 dude in this system, but Green might be my personal favorite. He has a chance to contribute in all five categories, with a plus batting average (a stat that has been exceedingly hard to find as of late). Because I'm typically one to value dynasty bats more than arms (really going out on a limb there), I'd have Green hovering around my personal top-20 list.

★ ★ ★ *2021 Top 101 Prospect* **#27** ★ ★ ★

3

Casey Mize   RHP   OFP: 60   ETA: Debuted in 2020
Born: 05/01/97   Age: 24   Bats: R   Throws: R   Height: 6'3"   Weight: 220
Origin: Round 1, 2018 Draft (#1 overall)

The Report: We really had no idea what to do with Mize last offseason. For the first half of 2019, he was the best pitching prospect in baseball, an absolute monster with a mid-90s fastball that he manipulated well and three plus off-speeds that all flashed plus-plus. The command was there and he looked like a potential future ace pitching in High-A and Double-A. Then he had a shoulder injury. While he came back briefly as a diminished version of himself and pitched poorly, he was quickly shut down after that, and we really didn't know what version of Mize to expect when the Tigers called him up in August.

Development Track: In Mize's first start in the majors, he flashed some of the ace potential, albeit with a little less command and a little less in-game endurance than you would have liked to see with all the question marks coming out of 2019. Those command and endurance issues lingered for his remaining six starts, and he also didn't always sit mid-90s as the season progressed. On balance, he was kind of terrible, and we're leaning a lot on our priors here to even have him this high.

Variance: High. Mize has shown us more than this in the past, and even flashed it for three and four inning spurts in the majors. He could put it back together very quickly—or never do so at all. I'd like to be optimistic here, but he really needs an uninterrupted season where nothing major goes wrong.

Mark Barry's Fantasy Take: Things were weird this year and everything should be taken with a grain of salt. Still, Mize was really bad in his debut, taking a huge step back with his command, failing to get many whiffs, and serving up dingers like they were macarons during Biscuit Week. Fold in his prior arm ailments and I am, as they say, worried. I'm in wait-and-see mode with Mize, so it's likely I won't have him on any fantasy teams in the near future.

★ ★ ★ *2021 Top 101 Prospect* **#46** ★ ★ ★

4

Matt Manning RHP   OFP: 60   ETA: 2021
Born: 01/28/98 Age: 23 Bats: R Throws: R Height: 6'6" Weight: 195
Origin: Round 1, 2016 Draft (#9 overall)

The Report: Manning profiles as a mid-rotation starting pitcher with some tantalizing hints that he might be even better. His fastball sits in the low-to-mid-90s, touching 96, and he gets great extension and angle on it. His power curveball profiles as a true plus pitch and flashes plus-plus potential, although it's a little humpier than you'd like. The changeup is going to make or break the profile as a starter; we projected that it would settle in as an average offering on balance last year, when it sometimes flashed higher and sometimes was too firm and looked like it needed to pick up a grade for him to stay in the rotation. Manning seems to have largely overcome past repeatability and delivery issues, and all-in-all he's a very fine pitching prospect.

Development Track: Manning probably would have debuted in the majors in 2020 were it not for a forearm strain. The Tigers shut him down in August, although we've been assured that he's healthy and ready to go for 2021. He was added to the 40-man roster after the season.

Variance: Medium, still. We still have concerns that he'll end up in the bullpen if the changeup consistency doesn't improve, and the forearm issues aren't exactly great. But there's positive variance here too, with his fastball/breaking ball combination hinting at higher-end outcomes if the rest sorts out.

Mark Barry's Fantasy Take: Potential mid-rotation starter, you say? With forearm issues? How could I possibly resist? As far as guys with that profile, however, I like Manning a little more than the rest. I think he'll strike enough guys out that he'll still be useful, even if the rate stats aren't great. He's an SP3 for me with the upside of a little more, but also a downside of a reliever.

——— ★ ★ ★ *2021 Top 101 Prospect* **#99** ★ ★ ★ ———

5 **Tarik Skubal LHP**   OFP: 55   ETA: Debuted in 2020
Born: 11/20/96   Age: 24   Bats: L   Throws: L   Height: 6'3"   Weight: 215
Origin: Round 9, 2018 Draft (#255 overall)

The Report: The Tigers made a bet on Skubal after he missed most of two college seasons following Tommy John surgery, and struggled with his control and command when he returned to the mound in 2018. It paid off in 2019, as a healthy Skubal dominated two levels with a plus fastball/slider combo. His Double-A K-rate was absurd, as he struck out nearly half of the Eastern League batters he faced. The raw pitch grades wouldn't suggest that level of dominance. His velocity is plus, but not spectacular when stretched out, and the fastball is high-spin but runs pretty true. The slider flashes plus-plus, but he can't always command it in a way that elicits chases against better hitters. But both pitches can play up to the deception and angle created in Skubal's delivery. There were still reliever markers even in his breakout campaign, but at worst we'd expect him to be a very good, potential multi-inning fireman.

Development Track: Skubal was promoted to Detroit the same week as Mize and Paredes. All three had their struggles adjusting to major league competition. Skubal leaned heavily on his fastball and hitters were able to hit it hard in the zone, although he got his fair share of swings-and-misses with it as well. They were able to lay off the slider and other secondaries enough to force Skubal into fastball counts, and it may not be enough fastball to turn over a lineup multiple times without further command and secondary improvement. He threw his change a lot, but it doesn't have a ton of action or deception, and his curveball is potentially average, but more a change-of-breaking-ball look for now. Despite the MLB struggles, we don't think the profile has changed all that much, although that multi-inning fireman role looks more likely.

Variance: Medium. The breaker is good enough you will find a role for him on a major-league staff, but the command, change, and durability issues mean it might be in a late-inning shutdown role.

Mark Barry's Fantasy Take: During his debut, Skubal's ERA more than doubled the second time through the order. It's a small sample, sure, but it's also the stuff multi-inning relievers are made of. It's too early to relegate him to that role (and the Tigers aren't good enough to have that pressing need), but his current profile is awfully Carlos Rodón-y and not in a good way.

6 Dillon Dingler C   OFP: 55   ETA: 2023
Born: 09/17/98 Age: 22 Bats: R Throws: R Height: 6'3" Weight: 210
Origin: Round 2, 2020 Draft (#38 overall)

The Report: You will be hard-pressed to find a player in the 2020 draft who improved his stock more given the very short season. After arriving at Ohio State as primarily a center fielder, the Buckeyes started to try him at catcher due to his overall athleticism. The transition to a full-time catcher role hit its peak this spring. Dingler showed an impressive ability to block pitches, flashed a plus arm, and demonstrated improved receiving. Not only did the defense now look above-average, so did his right-handed swing, as he consistently barreled balls while showing an advanced approach. Dingler is the rare projectable college catcher where both the offensive and defensive tools could end up above-average.

Development Track: Catching is still a relatively new position for Dingler. Even with the rapid improvements, he will need to continue to refine those skills and build upon them. He's a plus athlete for a backstop, which should help him handle the defensive rigors. The track record is limited yet promising, with reports out of post-draft workouts noting continued high performance.

Variance: Very High. All signs are trending upward, even if it is just a snapshot in time. There exists a scenario where the bat develops faster than the glove and you try to get him defensive reps a bunch of places. This could go in a bunch of different directions.

Mark Barry's Fantasy Take: Dingler could be very good, but as he's new to the position, it could take awhile. And that position is catcher. I don't think you have to take the plunge right away, and if he develops into the next, say, Daulton Varsho, then we'll cross that bridge when we come to it.

7 Isaac Paredes 3B   OFP: 50   ETA: Debuted in 2020
Born: 02/18/99 Age: 22 Bats: R Throws: R Height: 5'11" Weight: 213
Origin: International Free Agent, 2015

The Report: Since being acquired from the Cubs in 2017 Paredes has been a mainstay on the Tigers' list, ranking as high as third two years ago. The bat has always been the carrying tool and he's displayed the ability to hit at every level in his minor league tenure. There is plus raw power, but with the swing geared more for contact it plays average in game. Defensively, he's outgrown any possibility of sticking up the middle and has settled in at third base.

Detroit Tigers 2021

Development Track: Paredes started hot but never got back on track after a rough 1-for-29 late August slump. The final slash line (.220/.278/.290) was disappointing, but his youth and track record of hitting should give hope for a rebound. Detroit is in full rebuild mode and Paredes will get plenty of major league at bats next year.

Variance: Medium. This profile is tough when it's limited to a corner infield position. It's unlikely Paredes ever becomes a star, but his offensive game gives a pathway to a major league starting role.

Mark Barry's Fantasy Take: Lazy Teammate Comp Alert: the future fantasy line for Paredes reminds me a lot of Jeimer Candelario, which is also fun because they came over together from the Cubs. I'm still in for .280ish and 20 homers at peak, which is pretty useful, if not transcendent.

8. Alex Faedo   RHP   OFP: 50   ETA: 2021, if healthy
Born: 11/12/95   Age: 25   Bats: R   Throws: R   Height: 6'5"   Weight: 225
Origin: Round 1, 2017 Draft (#18 overall)

The Report: Faedo was one of the best pitchers in University of Florida history—he was the Most Outstanding Player of the 2017 College World Series—and was an early candidate to go first-overall in the 2017 MLB Draft. He fell to the middle of the round and has settled in as a good-not-great pitching prospect, but that's still fun. Faedo lives off a low-90s fastball and a plus slider that has been his go-to out pitch since college, and he commands and manipulates both pitches well. His changeup has lagged a bit behind, and that's the pitch he's going to need to improve to establish himself as a long-term starting option in the bigs. Given his fastball has touched higher velocities in the past and the quality of the slider, he should have a decent bullpen fallback, too.

Development Track: Faedo had a lost 2020, even by prospect standards; he tested positive for COVID-19 in July and was shut down for the season with a forearm strain not that long after he got ramped up at the alternate site. He was working out at instructs, and was added to the 40-man roster after the season.

Variance: Medium. We had "low" last year, and he hasn't actually pitched in games since then so there's no known additional talent variance or anything. But you really can't give a prospect low variance when he hasn't pitched since being shut down with a forearm strain.

Mark Barry's Fantasy Take: In this space last season, I had Faedo pegged as having fantasy SP5 upside. Since he pretty much hasn't pitched since then, I'm sticking to it.

9. Joey Wentz   LHP   OFP: 50   ETA: 2022
Born: 10/06/97   Age: 23   Bats: L   Throws: L   Height: 6'5"   Weight: 220
Origin: Round 1, 2016 Draft (#40 overall)

The Report: Wentz never consistently found the top-end, mid-90s velocity he showed as a prep his draft year, but after varying velocity reports and curveball effectiveness across his pro career, he had settled back in as a solid pitching prospect after being dealt to the Tigers at the 2019 deadline. A mechanical tweak upped the effectiveness of his low-90s fastball, and both the curve and change projected to above-average...

Development Track: ... and then Wentz was one of the handful of pitchers who blow out every spring, going under the knife for Tommy John surgery in March. His recovery is as expected so far and he should be back throwing in games by mid-season 2021. Perhaps this will allow him a reset from the past couple seasons of injury and inconsistency, but you never want to have major elbow surgery as a pitcher. Coming back 100 percent is not a guarantee as the surgery is common but not routine.

Variance: High. I suppose there are worse seasons to lose to a torn UCL and Tommy John, but even if Wentz has had a normal recovery so far, we won't know what he looks like until he's back on a mound next season.

Mark Barry's Fantasy Take: I'd keep a heralded southpaw on my watchlist as he treks back from Tommy John surgery, but I wouldn't go out and trade for such an arm.

10 Parker Meadows   CF   OFP: 50   ETA: 2023
Born: 11/02/99   Age: 21   Bats: L   Throws: R   Height: 6'5"   Weight: 205
Origin: Round 2, 2018 Draft (#44 overall)

The Report: Tall, lean, and athletic, Meadows has all the physical tools to be a top-flight center fielder. It takes a few steps for his 6-foot-5 frame to reach top gear, but when it does he has exceptional speed. Not the type of speed that will produce a ton of steals, but it will allow him to take extra bases and cover large swaths of ground in the outfield. He will grow into some power eventually as the swing develops.

Development Track: The lost season was particularly rough for Meadows. A solid year at Lakeland could have allowed us to chalk up his rough 2019 to the growing pains of a prep player in his first full season. We did get some good reports about his development during his brief stint at Toledo, but we will have to wait and see if real strides have been made offensively.

Variance: High. The athleticism and glove give him a path to the majors as a reserve type, but we're going to need to see him hit consistently if he's going to be anything more.

Mark Barry's Fantasy Take: I love the high ceiling for Meadows, but he's the type of prospect that suffers the most by missing out on competitive games. He still has a big ceiling, but without reps (and without steals), it's a fantasy risk I won't be taking.

The Prospects You Meet Outside The Top Ten

Prospects to dream on a little

Roberto Campos Born: 06/14/03 Age: 18 Bats: R Throws: R Height: 6'3" Weight: 200 Origin: International Free Agent, 2019
Campos is the Tigers' version of Jasson Dominguez without the Instagram highlights. Both signed their respective teams' largest international free agent contract and have yet to play stateside. Campos might not be as powerful as his Yankees counterpart, but reports tell of a similarly offensive-minded outfielder with a knack for barreling up the baseball. He's still just a teenager and until we get some live looks against real pitching, it's going to be a challenge to slot Campos into the prospect ranks.

Interesting Draft Follow

Gage Workman Born: 10/24/99 Age: 21 Bats: S Throws: R Height: 6'4" Weight: 195 Origin: Round 4, 2020 Draft (#102 overall)
Workman was the third baseman "blocking" Torkelson from playing there at Arizona State. He's a plus defender there with enough on-base skills due to a patient approach to be a useful left-side infield bench piece. He'll have to show a bit more pop to project as an everyday third baseman though.

Safe MLB bats, but less upside than you'd like

Daz Cameron CF Born: 01/15/97 Age: 24 Bats: R Throws: R Height: 6'2" Weight: 185 Origin: Round 1, 2015 Draft (#37 overall)
When the Tigers called Cameron up in September, I wrote much of our Call-Up article about his contact and plate approach issues. His swing and contact rates weren't *catastrophically* bad in his 59 PA late season run, but they weren't good either, and from an outcome perspective he walked only twice and struck out 19 times. The hit tool is the big question here; if he can hit .250 consistently the rest of the profile will carry him into being a good regular, but there's a lot of evidence he might not be able to hit .250 consistently without significant hit tool development.

Top Talents 25 and Under (as of 4/1/2021):

1. Spencer Torkelson, 3B/1B
2. Riley Greene, OF
3. Casey Mize, RHP
4. Matt Manning, RHP
5. Tarik Skubal, LHP

6. Dillon Dingler, C
7. Isaac Paredes, 3B
8. Alex Faedo, RHP
9. Joey Wentz, LHP
10. Willi Castro, SS

Willi Castro is the lone major-leaguer to make the list. The switch-hitting former Cleveland farmhand grabbed hold of the starting shortstop job in September and thrived, hitting .349 on the season with power over 140 plate appearances and ending up fourth in Rookie of the Year voting. While the performance was superficially impressive, his DRC+ was a mere 103, and his WARP was actually negative due to poor defensive performance. There's not a whole lot to suggest .349 with pop is attainable again and he's probably not really a shortstop, but there's a reasonable enough chance he levels out at useful or better to run it back in 2021.

Most of the rest of Detroit's top young talent is still prospect eligible. Other than Castro, the main player of note is Rony García, the top pick in the 2019 Rule 5 Draft who stuck on the roster all season. While I liked him some in the Yankees' system, he pitched very poorly in the majors and is not a better bet for long-term future success than Faedo or Wentz.

Part 3: Featured Articles

Tigers All-Time Top 10 Players

by Rob Mains

POSITION PLAYERS

HANK GREENBERG, 1B/OF (1930–1946)
Greenberg missed most of the 1936 season with a wrist injury inflicted by an opposing player, much of 1941 and 1945, and all of 1942-44, due to Word War II, so when looking at his accomplishments we have to imagine what his missing 4.5 seasons might have added to the portrait and then also figure in something ineffable for service to his country. He hit 41 homers and drove in 159 runs with a 1.103 OPS in 1939 and hit 44, drove in 127, and hit .977 the year after, so it's plausible to think he lost 200-plus homers and 550 or more RBI to the war. His 58 homers in 1938 have since been topped just once in the American League, by Roger Maris' 61 in '61, and his 184 RBI in 1937 are the third-most in MLB history. In 12 years with Detroit, he hit .319/.412/.616 with 306 homers and 1,200 RBI and he did it all while facing frequent slurs and, in 1938, a campaign by pitchers to keep a Jew from breaking Babe Ruth's record.

NORM CASH, 1B (1960–1974)
He came to Detroit via a trade with Cleveland for third baseman Steve Demeter, who went 0-for-5 with a strikeout for the rest of his career. Let's say Detroit won that one. Cash had an out-of-his-mind great year in in 1961, when he hit .361/.487/.662 with, it turned out later, a corked bat. He never approached those numbers again but he was a steady performer for 15 seasons for the Tigers, with consistently well-above-average batting numbers during the offense-starved 1960s. His 373 Tiger home runs are second only to Kaline. Once took a table leg up to bat against Nolan Ryan.

MIGUEL CABRERA, 1B/DH (2008–Present)

He won the triple Crown in 2012 and the "sabermetric triple crown" the year after, pacing the league in batting, on-base, and slugging. Another star first baseman who came to Detroit by way of a lopsided trade, this one from the Marlins after the 2007 season, his .931 OPS as a Tiger trails only Greenberg and Cobb. Miggy's slowed down in his old age, but he'll retire with 500 homers, a batting average over .300, an OPS over .900 and, eventually, a plaque in Cooperstown.

CHARLIE GEHRINGER, 2B (1925–1942)

In 16 seasons as a regular, all with Detroit, "The Mechanical Man" failed to hit .300 just three times. The finest player on the great Tigers teams of the 1930, in the 11 seasons from 1928 to 1938 he missed more than 10 games in a season only once and hit .331/.411/.502. He was a strong fielder and an outstanding hitter, batting third most of his career. He hit .371 in his 1937 MVP season and the year before he hit 60 doubles, the sixth-most ever.

LOU WHITAKER, 2B (1977–1995)

Sweet Lou has a plausible argument as the best player not in the Hall of Fame (non-steroid/disqualified division). He had a .789 career OPS, hit 244 homers, and walked more than he struck out, all while providing excellent defense at an up-the-middle position. He ranks fourth all-time for games played at second base. Between 1981 and 1989, he led American League second basemen in hits, homers, runs, and RBI. Aside from two 100-RBI seasons, Whitaker is missing many of the statistical markers which tickle the big-round-numbers fetish of small minds, but he was excellent nonetheless.

ALAN TRAMMELL, SS (1977–1996)

Whitaker's double-play partner didn't put together quite the same career numbers—not that a good-fielding shortstop who hits .285/.352/.415 needs any excuses. He was treated poorly by MVP voters during his career; he had a strong argument in 1984 and should have been a lock with his sensational 1987 (.343/.402/.551, 27 homers, 109 runs, 105 RBI). His 1984 postseason (.419/.500/.806) earned him World Series MVP, his only major award besides four Gold Gloves. The Trammell/Whitaker combo played together far longer than any other. They turned their first double play together in 1977 and their last 18 years later.

SAM CRAWFORD, OF (1903–1917)

Wahoo Sam (a comment not on his personality, but his hometown of Wahoo, Nebraska) broke into the majors in 1899 with the Cincinnati Reds but he jumped to the upstart American League after the 1902 season. He was an outstanding hitter, batting .309/.362/.452. Many of his all-time record of 309 triples likely would've been homers if he'd played in the lively ball era. Though they were longtime teammates, he and Ty Cobb were not friendly. Nevertheless, the Peach campaigned for Sam's enshrinement.

TY COBB, OF (1905–1926)

Between 1907 and 1925—19 years—the American League leader in OPS was Joe Jackson once, Tris Speaker once, Babe Ruth seven times, and Ty Cobb 10 times. He was 20 the first time he led the league and 38 the last time. He wasn't cuddly, but his reputation as a sociopath is largely a creation of a biographer who made up many of the stories about him. The Ty Cobb Healthcare System in Royston, Georgia was established via a $100,000 donation ($1.1 million in today's dollars) from Cobb to his hometown in 1950. In the hands of a less hackish writer, Cobb's famous intensity, partially derived from a family tragedy (his mother either murdered or accidentally killed his beloved father), might have been handled with empathy.

HARRY HEILMANN, OF (1914–1929)

"Slug" won four batting titles for the Tigers. He hit .403 in 1923, becoming the last American League hitter to top .400 until Ted Williams in 1941. His career .342 batting average is the seventh highest in league history. Between 1921 and 1927, he hit .380/.452/.583 and was the league's best hitter outside of Babe Ruth. After retiring after the 1932 season, he became the Tigers' radio broadcaster for 17 years.

AL KALINE, OF (1953–1974)

Mr. Tiger played 22 seasons in Detroit He was an All-Star in 15 of them, including 13 straight. He was a career .300 hitter until his last two seasons, at ages 38 and 39, pulled it down to .297, but he's the all-time Tigers leader in walks and homers. His .855 career OPS, adjusted for era, clocks in as the seventh-best in team history. He played an outstanding right field as well, winning 10 Gold Gloves.

PITCHERS

GEORGE MULLIN, RHP (1902–1913)

The durable Mullin pitched 260 or more innings nine straight years from 1902 to 1910, and had his best season (29-8, 2.22 ERA) for the pennant-winning 1909 Tigers. Detroit lost the World Series three straight years, from 1907 to 1909, but Mullin had a 1.86 ERA over six starts and a relief appearance in October. He holds the franchise record for innings and games started and had a career 2.76 ERA, second to Donovan, below, in franchise history.

WILD BILL DONOVAN, RHP (1903–1912, 1918)

His 2.49 ERA with the Tigers is the lowest among 24 Tigers pitchers who started at least 180 games for the club. The "wild" moniker came in his rookie season with the Washington Senators in 1898, when he walked 69 batters in 88 innings. In his Detroit years, though, he walked only one percent more batters than the league average. In his best season, 1907, he went 25-4 for the pennant-winning Tigers with a 2.19 ERA and followed that with an 18-7, 2.08 campaign in 1908. Had a subsequent career as a manager, during which he met a bad end in a train accident.

HOOKS DAUSS, RHP (1912–1926)

He spent his entire 15-year career with the Tigers. He's credited with the most wins in Detroit history, 223. As you could guess from his moniker, his out pitch was his curveball. He started 341 games and relieved 85 from 1913 to 1923, throwing 218 or more innings every season. Had many seasons in which he wasn't notably effective but hung in there anyway.

TOMMY BRIDGES, RHP (1930–1946)

Bridges was the top pitcher for the great Tigers teams of the mid-1930s. He's generously listed at 5'10", 155, but a devastating curveball made up for his small stature. He led the league in strikeouts twice and was in the top five seven of the eight years between 1933 and 1940. He got the Series-clinching win in Detroit's first world championship in 1935. He played his entire 16-year career in Detroit, and his 3.57 career ERA, while on the surface unremarkable, is the second-best in club history (after Newhouser, below) when adjusted for the high-offense era in which he pitched. A heavy workload in his 20s came home to roost in his 30s, but he was still able to pitch effectively in the Pacific Coast League for a few years after leaving the majors.

DIZZY TROUT, RHP (1939–1952)

Like Newhouser, his finest season was during World War II, as he went 27-14 in 1944 with a league-leading 2.12 ERA, 33 complete games, seven shutouts, and 352.1 innings pitched. He finished second to his teammate in the MVP vote, though he had more first-place votes and probably deserved the award. He's eighth in club history in starts and wins, seventh in innings, and sixth in shutouts. His park- and era-adjusted ERA is third only to Newhouser and Bridges among Tigers. That he lasted 15 seasons is something of a miracle given how many times he nearly wore out his welcome with outbursts of various kinds.

HAL NEWHOUSER, LHP (1939–1953)

One of just 13 players to win back-to-back MVPs, Newhouser sometimes gets shortchanged because his MVP years were during World War II (1944-5). But in 1946, he led the league with 26 wins and a 1.94 ERA, finishing second to Ted

Williams in the MVP vote. He was an outstanding pitcher in 1947 and 1948 as well, but went only 38-29 due to a lack of run support. The mercurial Detroit native was excused from military service due to a mitral valve prolapse but he tried repeatedly to enlist. Instead, he stayed stateside, leading the league in wins four times and ERA twice.

MICKEY LOLICH, LHP (1963–1975)
The portly portsider played second fiddle to Denny McLain early in his career but emerged as one of baseball's most resilient starters, averaging over 300 innings per year from 1969 to 1974, including 376 in 1971, the second-most in MLB since 1917. An inconsistent starter in his early years, he was banished to the bullpen for part of the 1968 season but came back to win World Series MVP, pitching three complete game victories, the last, in Game 7, on two days' rest.

JOHN HILLER, LHP (1965–1980)
Hiller began his 15-season career, all with Detroit, as a swingman, starting 31 games and relieving 124 from 1965 to 1970 with a nifty 2.98 ERA. But on January 11, 1971, he suffered three heart attacks, putting his career in jeopardy. He became a minor league instructor but was called into active duty to shore up a struggling Tigers bullpen in 1972. He went on to pitch nine more seasons. He was a workhorse out of the bullpen, surpassing 120 innings four times. In 1973, he posted a 1.44 ERA and led the league with 38 saves, whiffing 124 batters in 125.1 innings. It remains on the shortlist for best pure relief season in history.

JACK MORRIS, RHP (1977–1990)
Many remember him for his 1991 World Series performance with the Twins, but he played 14 of his 18 seasons in Detroit. He's a marginal Hall of Famer because of his 3.90 career ERA (3.73 with the Tigers) but he ranks fourth all-time in innings for the Tigers, second in games started, and fifth in wins, with 198. His postseason heroics also predated his time in Minnesota. He won the opener of Detroit's sweep of the Royals in the 1984 ALCS and pitched complete games in the first and fourth games of the World Series, winning both.

JUSTIN VERLANDER, RHP (2005–2017)
His 12-plus seasons in Detroit were littered with accolades: Rookie of the Year in 2006, Cy Young Award and MVP in 2011, six-time All-Star, led the league in wins twice, innings three times, and strikeouts four times. His trade to the Astros in 2017 is something Tigers fans would rather forget, but perhaps they'll see him wearing a Tigers cap again when he's called up to Cooperstown.

A Taxonomy of 2020 Abnormalities

by Rob Mains

I'm going to start this with a trivia question. Trust me, it's relevant. Don't bother skipping to the end of the article to find the answer, it's not there.

Only five players have appeared in 140 or more games for 16 straight seasons. Who are they?

It's a trivia question starting off an essay, so you know how this works: Whatever you guessed, you're wrong. It's okay. As someone who purchased this book, chances are good that you're an educated baseball fan. But the circumstances behind 2020 force us to abandon, or at least seriously question, some of our favorite patterns and crutches for evaluating the game we love.

We just completed what was undoubtedly the strangest season in MLB history. No fans, geographically limited schedule, universal DH, seven-inning twin bills, runners on second in extra innings, a 16-team postseason, a club playing at a Triple-A stadium. Some of these changes will likely persist (sorry), but we've never had so many tweaks dumped on us all at once, at least not since they figured out how many balls were in a walk.

And the biggest, of course, was the 60-game season. The 19th century was dotted with teams that went bankrupt before the season ended, but the lone season with only 60 scheduled games was 1877. That year there were only six teams, the league rostered a total of 77 players (just 16 more than the 2020 Marlins), and batters called for pitches to be thrown high or low by the pitcher, who was 50 feet away. We can say the 2020 season was easily the shortest ever for recognizable baseball.

As such, it'll stand out. Few abbreviated seasons do. Just about everybody reading this knows the 1994 season ended after Seattle's Randy Johnson struck out Oakland's Ernie Young for the last out of the Mariners-A's game on August 11. The ensuing player strike wiped out the rest of the season and the postseason. Teams played only 112-117 games that year.

And many of you know that a strike in the middle of the 1981 season split the season in two, resulting in the only Division Series until 1995. Teams played only 103-111 games that year, the shortest regular season since 1885.

Those two seasons are memorable. So when we see that nobody drove in 100 runs in 1981, or that Greg Maddux was the only pitcher with 180 or more innings pitched in 1994, we think, "Of course. Strike year."

But we don't remember other short years. You might not recall that the 1994 strike spilled into the next year, chopping 18 games off the 1995 schedule. You might've read that the 1918 season, played during the last pandemic, ended after Labor Day due to the government's World War I "work or fight" order. A strike erased the first week and a half of the 1972 season, but that year's best known as the last time pitchers batted in the American League.

The point is, while we don't remember small changes to the schedule, we remember the big ones. The 1981 mid-season strike. The 1994 season- and Series-ending strike. And, of course, the pandemic-shortened 2020 season. We won't need a reminder why Marcell Ozuna's 18 homers were the fewest to lead the National League in a century. (Literally; Cy Williams led with 15 in 1920.)

Now, about that trivia question. The five players are Hank Aaron, Brooks Robinson, Pete Rose, Ichiro Suzuki, and Johnny Damon. The one nobody gets, of course, is Damon, and a lot of people miss Ichiro, whose last season of 140-plus games came garbed in the red-orange and ocean blue of Miami when he was 42. That's half of what makes it a good question. The other half is the two guys whom many think made the list but didn't. Lou Gehrig? His streak started in the Yankees' 42nd game of the 1925 season and lasted only 13 seasons after that. And everybody assumes Cal Ripken Jr. did it, having played 2,632 straight games over 17 seasons. But one of those 17 seasons was 1994, when the Orioles played only 112 games.

My point? *I just told you* everybody remembers the 1994 strike year, but everybody forgets it fell in the middle of Ripken's streak, separating the first twelve years from the last four. Just because we recall something doesn't mean it's always at the front of our minds.

Nobody is going to forget 2020, and baseball is obviously not the main reason. But there will come a time in the future when you're looking at a player's or a team's record, and there will be baffling numbers there for 2020, and you'll think, "I wonder what happened." (Not to mention the missing line for minor league players.) Just like you forgot that the 1994 strike limited Ripken to 112 games.

Try not to forget it, though. The 2020 season resulted in weird statistical results for several reasons.

There were only 60 games.
I know, duh. But that had impacts beyond counting stats like Ozuna's home run total or Yu Darvish and Shane Bieber leading the majors with eight wins. (I know, pitcher wins, but still.)

The 162-game season is the longest among major North American sports, and that duration gives us a gift. Over the course of a long season, small variations tend to even out. A player who has a ten-game hot streak will probably have a ten-game cold streak. A team that starts the year losing a bunch of close games will probably win a bunch of them. We get regression to the mean. Statistics stabilize.

Consider flipping a coin. Over the long run, we expect it to come up heads about half the time. But the fewer flips, the more variation there'll be. If you flip a coin six times, probability theory tells us you'll get at least two-third heads about 34 percent of the time. Flip it 30 times, your chance of two-thirds heads drops to five percent.

Or, relevant to this case, if you flip a coin 60 times, your chance of getting at least 36 heads—that's 60 percent—is 7.75 percent. Expand the coin-flipping to 162 times, and the chance of getting 60 percent heads drops to 0.73 percent.

In other words, the odds of an outcome that's 20 percent better (or worse) than expected is *more than ten times higher* when you flip your coin 60 times than when you do it 162 times. Call it small sample size, call lack of mean reversion, or call it luck not evening out, 162 is a lot more predictive than 60. You get much more variation over 60 games than over 162. Bieber's 1.63 ERA and 0.87 FIP aren't something we'd see over a full season, and neither is Javier Baéz's .203/.238/.360.

Some players' lines in 2020 look normal. Brian Anderson had an .811 OPS in 2019 and an .810 OPS in 2020. (He probably would have gotten that last point if he'd been given enough time.) But there are many like Bieber and Baéz, some of them young players still establishing their talent levels. The answer to the question, "What went right or wrong for that guy in 2020?" is most likely "Nothing, it was just a 2020 thing."

Preseason training was abbreviated for hitters.

Every year, spring training drags. Players get tired of it, fans get tired of it, and you sure can tell sportswriters get tired of it. Yes, something to get everyone into shape is necessary, but does it really have to drag on for over a month? Can't we shorten it?

The 2020 season answered in the negative, at least for hitters. Warren Spahn is credited with saying that hitting is timing and pitching is upsetting timing. It appears nobody had his timing down after the abbreviated July summer camp. Through August 9—18 games into the season—MLB batters were hitting .230/.311/.395 with a .275 BABIP. That BABIP, had it held, would have been the lowest since 1968, the Year of the Pitcher. In recent years it's hovered around .300.

It didn't hold. Play returned to more normal levels the rest of the year: .249/.325/.425 with a .297 BABIP starting August 10. But batters whose play concentrated in those first two weeks wound up with ugly lines. Andrew

Benintendi went on the injured list with a season-ending rib cage strain on August 11. His final line: .103/.314/.128 in 14 games. Franchy Cordero went on the IL with a hamate bone fracture on August 9 and a .154/.185/.231 line. Even though he came back strong in a late September return, it was too late to repair his full-season numbers.

Preseason training was abbreviated for pitchers.

Every year, spring training drags. Players get tired of it, fans get tired of it ... wait, I already said that. But the abbreviated preseason was tough on pitchers, too. As noted, they had the upper hand coming out of the gate. But then they lost that hand. And then their arms, too.

The 2020 season was spread over 67 days. During those 67 days, 237 pitchers hit the Injured List, compared to 135 in the first 67 days of 2019. A lot of those IL stints, though, were COVID-19-related. Still, over the first 67 days of the 2019 season, there were 72 pitchers on the IL with arm injuries. That figure jumped to 110 in 2020, a 53 percent increase.

There are a number of factors contributing to pitcher arm injuries, ranging from usage to velocity, but it appears that attenuated preseason training played a role. A lot of pitchers had super-short seasons due to arm woes. Corey Kluber, Roberto Osuna, and Shohei Ohtani combined for seven innings, none after August 8. All suffered arm injuries. We'll never know whether they'd have fared better with a longer preseason, but we can guess how they probably feel.

Everybody played.

Rosters were set to expand from 25 to 26 in 2020, so even if we'd had a normal season, we'd have likely seen 2019's record of 1,410 players on MLB rosters broken. But due to the pandemic, rosters started the year at 30 and were cut to only 28. Add multiple COVID-19 absences and the revolving door caused by poor starts by hitters and a rash of pitcher arm injuries, and 1,289 players appeared in MLB games in 2020. The comparable figure over the first 67 days of the 2019 season was 1,109. That 16 percent increase works out to an average of six more players per team in 2020 compared to a similar slice of 2019. A future look back at 2020 rosters will include a lot of unfamiliar names.

Plus became a minus.

In advanced metrics, we adjust batter and pitcher performance for park and league/era variations. A plus sign appended to the end of a measure means that it's adjusted for park and league. It's scaled to an average of 100, with higher figures above average and lower figures below average. (Similarly, a metric with a minus is also park- and league-adjusted and scaled to 100, with lower values better.) Here at BP, our advanced measure of offensive performance is DRC+. Baseball-Reference has OPS+ and FanGraphs has wRC+.

Using park and league adjustments, we can compare Dante Bichette's 1995 Steroid Era season at pre-humidor Coors Field (.340/.364/.620, 40 homers, 128 RBI, MVP runner-up) with Jim Wynn's 1968 Year of the Pitcher season at the cavernous Astrodome (.269/.376/.474, 26 homers, 67 RBI, no MVP votes). It's not close. DRC+, OPS+, and wRC+ all give the nod to Wynn, handily. This is a useful tool. As my Baseball Prospectus colleague Patrick Dubuque tweeted last fall, "Please note that when I ask how you are, I am already adjusting for era."

The 2020 season messes up plus (and minus) stats for two reasons. First, the park adjustment was based on only 30 home games instead of the usual 81. Everything noted above regarding the short season applies, literally doubly, to park effect calculations. DRC+ uses a single-season park factor. OPS+ uses a three-year average and wRC+ five years. The figure for 2020 is suspect.

Second, OPS+ and wRC+ adjust for league: American and National. (DRC+ adjusts for opponent, regardless of league.) While there were two leagues in 2020, they were an artificial construct. To reduce travel, teams played opponents geographically, not based on league. There weren't two leagues, American and National. There were three, Western, Central, and Eastern.

That makes a difference because teams in the same league played in different run-scoring environments. AL teams scored 4.58 runs per game, NL teams 4.71. That's a small difference. But teams in the East scored 0.21 more runs per game (4.95) than teams in the West (4.74), and they both scored a lot more than Central teams (4.25). Adjusting for league misses that difference, so this book will be safe in that regard, but other sources may be distorted somewhat.

Not every game was a "game."
In 2020, the rising tide of strikeouts was finally stemmed. Strikeouts per team per game fell from 8.8 in 2019 to 8.7 in 2020. That marked the first decline after 14 straight annual increases.

In 2020, the rising tide of strikeouts rose higher. Batters struck out in 23.4 percent of plate appearances compared to 23.0 percent in 2019. That marked the 15th straight annual increase.

Both are true statements.

Because of two rule changes—seven-inning doubleheaders and runners on second in extra innings—games in 2020 were unprecedented in their brevity. There were 37.0 plate appearances per game in 2020. The only years with fewer were 1904 and 1906-1909. The average game in 2020 entailed 8.61 innings pitched, the fewest since 1899.

So when you see any per-game stats for 2020, you need to increase them by 3 or 4 percent to get them on equal footing with recent years.

Or, better, just ignore them. Last year happened. There were major league games contested between major league teams. But when you're looking at those physical or electronic baseball cards, when you're weaving narratives over why this young player's inevitable rise to stardom fell apart or why that old veteran rekindled his magic, don't linger on the 2020 line. It was just too weird.

Thanks to Lucas Apostoleris for research assistance.

—*Rob Mains is an author of Baseball Prospectus.*

Tranches of WAR

by Russell A. Carleton

We ask "replacement level" to be a lot of things. Sometimes contradictory things. Sometimes I wonder if we know what it even means anymore. The original idea was that it represented the level of production that a team could expect to get from "freely available talent", including bench players, minor leaguers, and waiver wire pickups. It created a common benchmark to compare everyone to, and for that reason, it represented an advancement well beyond what was available at the time. In fact, it created a language and a framework for evaluating players that was not just better but *entirely* different than what came before it.

But then we started mumbling in that language. The idea behind "wins above replacement" was one part sci-fi episode and one part mathematical exercise. Imagine that a player had disappeared before the season and suddenly, in an alternate timeline, his team would have had to replace him. The distance between him and that replacement line was his value. We need to talk about that alternate timeline.

Without getting too into 2:00 am "deep conversations" with extensive navel-gazing, it's worth thinking about why one player might not be playing, while another might.

- A player might not be playing because he has a short-term injury or his manager believes that he needs a day off.
- A player might not be playing because he has a longer-term injury that requires him to be on the injured list.

There's a difference here between these two situations. In particular, the first one generally *doesn't* involve a compensatory roster move, while the second one does. It's possible, though not guaranteed, that the person who will be replacing the injured/resting player would be the same in either case. That matters. Teams generally carry a spare part for all eight position players on the diamond, although in the era of a four-player bench, those spare parts usually are the backup plan for more than one spot.

Detroit Tigers 2021

A couple of years ago, I posed a hypothetical question. Suppose that a team had two players in its system fighting for a fourth outfielder spot. One of them was a league average hitter, but would be worth 20 runs below average if allowed to play center field for a full season. One of them was a perfectly average fielder, but would be 15 runs below average as a hitter, if allowed to play an entire season. Which of the two should the team roster? It's tempting to say the second one, as overall, he is the better player. That misses the point. A league average hitter on the bench isn't just a potential replacement for an injured outfielder. He might also pinch hit for the light-hitting shortstop in a key spot. You keep the average hitter on the roster, even though he isn't a hand-in-glove fit for one specific place on the field, because being a bench player is a different job description than being a long-term fill-in for someone. If you find yourself in need of a longer-term fill-in, you can bring the other guy up from AAA.

When we're determining the value of an everyday player though, if he had disappeared before the season and a team would have had to replace his production, they likely would have done it with a player who was a long-term fill-in type because they would have had to replace a guy who played everyday. Maybe that's the same guy that they would have rostered on their bench anyway, but we don't know. It gets to the query of what we hope to accomplish with WAR. Are we looking for an accurate modeling of reality or are we looking for a common baseline to compare everyone to? Both have their uses, but they are somewhat different questions.

Let's talk about another dichotomy.

- A player might not be playing because he isn't very good and is a bench-level player.
- A player might not be playing because there is another player on the team who has a situational advantage that makes him the better choice today. The classic case of this is a handedness platoon. On another day, he might be a better choice.

When we think about player usage, I think we're still stuck in the model that there are starters and there are scrubs. We have plenty of words for bench players or reserves or backups or utility guys. We do still have the word "platoon" in our collective vocabulary, but in the age of short benches, it's hard to construct one. It's always been hard to construct them. You have to find two players who hit with different hands, have skill sets that complement each other, and probably play the same position. In the era of the short bench, one of them had probably better double as a utility player in some way. Baseball has a two-tiered language geared toward the idea of regulars and reserves. The fact that it was so easy for me to find plenty of synonyms for "a player whose primary function is to come into a game to replace a regular player if he is injured or resting" should tell you something.

I'm always one to look for "unspoken words" in baseball. What is it called when someone is both half of a platoon and the utility infielder? That guy exists sometimes, but he reveals himself in that role—usually by accident. We don't have a word for that, and whenever I find myself saying "we don't have a word for that", I look for new opportunities. What do you call it, further, when the job of being the utility infielder is decentralized across the whole infield with occasional contributions from the left fielder? It's not even a "super-utility" player. What happens when you build your entire roster around the idea that everyone will be expected to be a triple major?

⚾ ⚾ ⚾

I think someone else beat me to this one, and on a grand scale. Platoons work because we know that hitters of the opposite hand to the pitcher get better results than hitters of the same hand, usually to the tune of about 20 points of OBP. If you want to express that in runs, it usually comes out to somewhere around 10 to 12 runs of linear weights value prorated across 650 PA. But hang on a second, now let's say that we have two players who might start today, both of roughly equal merit with the bat. One has a handedness advantage, but is the worse fielder of the two. In that case, as long as his "over the course of a season" projection as a fielder at whatever position you want to slot him into is less than a 10-run drop from the guy he might replace, then he's a better option today.

We're not used to thinking of utility players as bat-first options, who would play below-average defense at three different infield positions. That guy might hook on as a 2B/3B/LF type (Howie Kendrick, come on down!) but teams usually think to themselves that they need as their utility infielder someone who "can handle" shortstop, the toughest of the infield spots to play. If someone can do that *and* hit well, he's probably already starting somewhere, so he's not available as a utility infielder. It's easier for those glove guys to find a job. In a world where the replacement for a shortstop *has to be* the designated utility infielder, that makes sense.

But as we talked about last week, we're living in a different world. The rate at which a replacement for a regular starter turns out to be *another starter* shifting over to cover has gone way up over the last five years. There was always some of it in the game, but this has been a supernova of switcheroos. Now if your second baseman is capable of playing a decent shortstop, that 2B/3B/LF guy can swap in. He's not actually playing shortstop, and maybe the defense suffers from the switch, but if he's got enough of a bat, he might outhit those extra fielding miscues. And in doing so, he is effectively your backup shortstop.

Somewhere along the lines, teams got hip to the idea of multi-positional play from their regulars. I've written before about how you can't just put a player, however athletic, into a new position and expect much at first. The data tell us that. Eventually, players can learn to be multi-positionalists, but it takes time, roughly on the order of two months, before they're OK. But there's a hidden message in there. If you give a player some reps at a new spot, he's a reasonably gifted athlete and somewhat smart and willing to learn, he could probably pick it up enough to get to "good enough," and it doesn't take forever. You just have to be purposeful about it. Maybe you get to the point where you can start to say "he's still below average but we could move him there and get another bat into the lineup, and it's a net win."

Teams have started to build those extra lessons into their player development program. It used to be seen as a mark of weakness to be relegated to "utility player" because that meant that you were a bench player (all those synonyms above come with a side of stigma). Now, it's a way of building a team. If you get a few reps in the minors (where it doesn't count) at a spot, you'll have at least played the spot at game speed before. There are limits to how far you can push that. A slow-footed "he's out in left field because we don't have the DH" guy is never going to play short, but maybe your third baseman can try second base and not look like a total moose out there.

⚾ ⚾ ⚾

Back to WAR. I'd argue that the world of starters and scrubs is slowly disintegrating, for good cause. In the event that a regular starter really does go down with an injury–ostensibly, the alternate universe scenario that WAR is attempting to model–it makes the team a little more resilient to replacing him. And the good news is that you're more likely to be able to replace him with the best of the bench bunch, rather than the third-best guy, because the best guy doesn't have to be an exact positional match for the guy who got hurt. And that's what the manager would want to do. He'd want to replace that long-term production, not with an amalgam of everyone else who played that position, but with the best guy available from his reserves.

Now this is still WAR. We still want to retain the principle that we should be measuring a player, and not his teammates. We need some sort of common baseline, and despite what I just said, we'll still need some sort of amalgam. To construct that, I give to you the idea of the tranche. The word, if you've not heard it before, refers to a piece of a whole that is somehow segmented off. It's often used in finance to talk about layers of a financial instrument.

Here, I want you to consider that there are 30 starters at each of the seven non-battery positions (catchers should have their own WAR, since only a catcher can replace a catcher). We can identify them by playing time, and we can futz around with the definition a little bit if we need to. Next, among those who aren't in that starting pool, we identify the top tranche of the 30 best bench players, which I would again identify by playing time, and then the second and third and fourth and so on. If a player were to disappear, his manager would probably want to take a guy from that top tranche of the bench to replace him. In a world where even the starters can slide around the field, that becomes more feasible.

We can take a look at that top tranche and say "How many of them showed that they are able to play (first, second, etc.)?" and therefore could have directly substituted for the starter? How many of them could have been a direct substitute for our injured player? We don't know whether one of them would be on *a specific* team, but we can say that 40 percent of the time, a manager would have been able to draw from tranche 1 in filling the role, and 35 percent from tranche 2. But on tranche 1, we can also look at how many of those players played a position that could have then shifted and covered for that spot. We'd need some eligibility criteria for all of this (probably a minimum number of games played) but it would just be a matter of multiplication. Shortstop would be harder to fill, and managers would probably be dipping a little further down in the talent pool, and so replacement level would be lower, as it is now.

Doing some quick analysis, I found that the difference in just batting linear weights (haven't even gotten into running or fielding) between tranche 1 and tranche 2 in 2019 was about 6.5 runs, prorated across 650 PA. Between tranche 1 and tranche 3, it's 10.8 runs. The ability to shift those plate appearances up the ladder has some real value.

This part is important. We can also give credit to starters for the positions that they showed an ability to play, even if they didn't play them (this is the guy fully capable of playing center, but who's in a corner because the team already has a good center fielder) because he allows a team to carry a player who hits like a left fielder to functionally be the team's backup center fielder. He facilitates that movement upward among the tranches. We can start to appreciate the difference between a left fielder who would never be able to hack it in center (and the compensatory move that his team would have to make) and the left fielder who could do it, but just didn't have to very often.

Past that, you can continue to use whatever hitting and fielding and running metrics you like to determine a player's value, but when we get down to constructing that baseline, I'd argue we need a better conceptual and mathematical framework. It's going to require some more #GoryMath than we're used to, but I'd argue it's a better conceptualization of the way that MLB actually plays the game in 2020. If…y'know…MLB plays in 2020. If WAR is going to be our flagship statistic among the *acronymati*, then we need to acknowledge that it contains some old and starting-to-be-out-of-date assumptions about the game. We may need to tinker with it. Here's my idea for how.

—*Russell A. Carleton is an author of Baseball Prospectus.*

Secondhand Sport

by Patrick Dubuque

Back before time stopped, I liked to go to thrift stores. Now that I'm older, I rarely ever buy anything—I don't need much in my life, now—but I still enjoy the old familiar circuit: check to see if there are baseball cards to write about, look for board or card games to play with the kids, scan for random ironic jerseys, hit the book section. It takes ten, maybe fifteen minutes. Thrift stores are the antithesis of modern online shopping, because you don't know what they have, and you don't even really know what you want. It's junk, literal junk, stuff other people thought was worthless. That's what makes it great.

In an idealized economy, thrift stores shouldn't exist. Everybody has a living wage, and every product has a durability that exactly matches its desired life; nothing should need to be given away, no one should need to be given to. But then, thrift stores shouldn't work on a customer experience level, either. You wouldn't think an ethos of "let's make everything disorganized and hard to find" would lead to customer satisfaction, but low-budget retailers like TJ Maxx and Ross thrive on this model. People like bargain hunting as much for the hunting as the bargain; it's part of the experience, spending time as if it's a wager. There's a thrill, occasionally, in inefficiency.

In sports, the modern overuse of the word "inefficiency" is a condemnation: It insinuates that there is *an* efficiency, a correct way to be found, and that all other ways are wrong ways. It's prevalent in baseball but hardly contained to it; the lifehack, the Silicon Valley disruption are other examples of productivity creep in our daily lives. Their modern success makes plenty of sense. Maximization of resources, after all, is its own puzzle, and an industry of European board games is founded upon it. It's fun to take a system and optimize it, unravel it like a sudoku puzzle. If there's only one kind of genius, after all, there's no way anyone can fail to appreciate it.

Baseball has been hacking away at these perceived inefficiencies since its inception: platoons, bullpens, farm systems were all installed to extract more out of the tools at hand. But it's been a particular badge of the sabermetric movement, from Ken Phelps and his All-Star Team to Ricardo Rincon and the darlings of *Moneyball*. It's business, but it's also an ethos: the idea that there's treasure among the trash, something we all failed to appreciate until someone brought it to light.

It's the myth that made Sidd Finch so enticing, that fuels so many "best shape" narratives and new pitch promises. We all, athletes and unathletic sportswriters, want to believe that there's genius trapped inside us, and that it's just a matter of puzzling out the combination to unlock it. That our art, our style is the next inefficiency, waiting for our own Billy Beane. It's why we root for underdogs, and why we're excited for the Mike Tauchmans and the Eurubiel Durazos, champions of skin-deep mediocrity.

Except we aren't anymore, really. The days of "Free X" have descended beyond the ring of irony and into obscurity. There are still Xs to be freed, or at least one X, duplicated endlessly: Mike Ford, Luke Voit, Max Muncy. The undervalued one-dimensional slugger demonstrated how the game hasn't quite culturally caught up to its logical extreme. But for those who don't fit the rather spacious mold, times are grimmer. As Rob Arthur revealed several months ago, there's been a marked increase in the number of sub-replacement relievers. It's the outcome of a greater number of teams forced to play out games without the talent to win them, but it's also emblematic of the modern tendency of teams to dispose of their disposable assets, burning through cost-controlled arms the way that man chopped down forests in *The Lorax*. Stuff just isn't built to outlive their original owners anymore.

It's unsurprising, given how well-mined the market for inefficiencies has been of late. The disciples of the early analytics departments, and the disciples of those, have proliferated the league, with only a few backwater holdouts. The league has grown smarter, but every team has learned the same lesson. In fact, the phenomenon creates a peculiar kind of feedback loop: As teams value a specific subset of players or skills, prospective athletes learn to increase their own marketability by conforming themselves to the demands of their prospective employers.

And that's tragic, in the way that the extinction of animals is tragic; a certain amount of biodiversity in baseball has been lost. Shortstops hit like outfielders. Pitchers don't hit at all. Only the catchers remain idiosyncratic, thanks to the defensive demands of their position; eventually they too will be required to produce like everyone else, or they'll meet the fate of their battery mates. A perfect economy requires perfect production.

I mentioned earlier that more and more, I leave thrift stores empty-handed. It is true that I am more discerning than in the past; my bookshelves are full, and there are more streaming films than I will ever be able to watch. But there are other factors at play.

Thrift stores are, in a way, the bond markets of retail. When the economy is rough and other retailers are struggling, more people look secondhand for their products. But as recently as last year, publications were noting a reversal of the trend: Companies like Goodwill and Savers were expanding despite a strong economy. Publications credited a heightened sense of environmentalism and a rejection of cutting-edge fashion as drivers behind the increase, though the more likely answer is the modern American economy hasn't showered its favors equally, particularly among the young.

But it is more than just the economy. Baseball and thrift stores share something else in common, evident in our current conversations about restarting the sport: They live in the gray area between public service and private enterprise. Thrift stores provide affordable necessities to lower-class citizens, and collectibles and fashion for the middle-class. Because of the success of the latter, prices have gone up across the board. Especially in terms of clothing, the middle-class flight from fashion into vintage has instead carried the aftereffects of fashion, including its costs, into a territory where people just want clothes. But there's another factor in the rise of prices, in the form of the internet.

The Goodwills of the world have grown smarter, too, employing the internet to extract full value from their detritus. Ebay, similarly, has lost much of the charm it had as a new frontier around the turn of the century. Everything has a price point now; even individual taste is no match for the algorithm, because anything rare, no matter how niche its market, is a collectible to someone.

The internet has had the same effect on thrift stores that sabermetrics has had on baseball; its equivalent to OBP was the bar scanner. As detailed in Slate, the rise of second-party stores on eBay and Amazon birthed an entire industry of used-good salespeople, armed with PDAs and scanners, buying books for three dollars to sell online for five. The author, Michael Savitz, reports earning $60,000 by working nearly 80 hours a week; he makes it clear that this is not a vocation of his choosing. It's long hours, with no real creativity or individuality, skimming the cream off of a local establishment and flipping it to someone with a little more money on the other side of the country. And once the vocation exists, the obvious question arises: why wait to put the wares out on the shelves? Why allow value to exist at all?

Nothing is ruined. Thrift stores will continue to sell polo shirts and DVDs, and baseball will continue to exist and make or lose money, depending on who you believe. But as we continue to refine our knowledge, we lose something in the conquest for efficiency, a delight born out of the unknown. The problem isn't the efficiency itself; we can't blame the booksellers, or the people sweeping freeways to collect grams of platinum from damaged catalytic converters. The problem is a system that requires this sort of profit-skimming behavior in order to feed families (or, for corporations, maximize shareholder return).

In times like these, with the 2020 season on the brink and the collective bargaining agreement close behind, it can often feel like the current situation is untenable. It can't keep going like this, even if we don't know what to do about it. But as with thrift stores, there's an equally irresistible feeling that it *has* to keep going, that it would be unimaginable to not have this broken, amazing sport. Both industries exist on an invisible foundation of friction, of chaos and unpredictability, even as both see their foundations buffed down to a perfect, untouchable polish. But if COVID-19 and its financial ramifications do, as some have suggested, make it such that the baseball that returns is fundamentally different than the baseball that came before, perhaps this is the time to lean in, and change the game even more. Fix bunting. Make defense more difficult. Create viable, alternate strategies. Add some chaos back into baseball. It's fun when no one knows quite where things are.

—*Patrick Dubuque is an author of Baseball Prospectus.*

Steve Dalkowski Dreaming

by Steven Goldman

We dream of being a pitcher, of starring in the major leagues. Depending on your age and your sense of historical perspective, you might imagine yourself as Walter Johnson, throwing harder than anyone else—hitting more batters than anyone else, too, but always feeling bad about it. You could picture yourself as a Tom Seaver or a David Cone, with all the stuff in the world but still being cerebral about it, thinking about so much more than burning 'em in there. There are so many models one could choose: You could be a Lefty Gomez, Jim Bouton, or Bill Lee, skilled, but not taking the whole thing too seriously, or a Lefty Grove, Bob Gibson, or Steve Carlton, powerful but treating each start like a mission to be survived instead of a game to be enjoyed.

Very few would dream of being Steve Dalkowski, the former Baltimore Orioles prospect who died of COVID-19 last week at the age of 80. Yet, there is something just as noble in Dalkowski's negative accomplishments—and accomplishments is what they are—as there is in the precision-engineered pitching of a Greg Maddux. You have to be very good to be that bad. Dalkowski had all of the stuff of the greatest pitchers but none of the command; his story is not one of failing to conquer his limitations, but striving against one of the cruelest hands that fate or genetics or personality can deal us: A desire to achieve great things which is almost but not quite matched by the ability to meet that goal.

As with Johnson, Grove, Bob Feller, and the rest of the hard-throwing pitchers who played before the advent of modern radar guns, we have to take the word of the players and coaches who saw Dalkowski pitch as to his velocity. He was a hard-drinking, maximum-effort pitcher who, if their memories are to be believed, consistently threw over 100 miles per hour. His was the Maltese Fastball, the stuff that dreams are made of. The problem is that velocity without command and control is still a good distance from utility. Dalkowski was the most effective towel you could design for a fish, the sleekest bathing suit intended to be worn by an astronaut, but that doesn't mean he wasn't beautiful: We can appreciate a journey even if it doesn't end at the intended destination.

Whether because of sloppy mechanics he couldn't calm, an inability to understand that a consistent 98 in the strike zone would likely be more effective than a consistent 110 out of it, or all that beer, Dalkowski could never make the adjustments that pitchers like Feller and Nolan Ryan made before him, possibly because he had so far to go: Feller, who never pitched in the minors, came up at 17 and spent three years walking almost seven batters per nine innings before settling in at 3.8 beginning when he was 20. Ryan started out walking over six batters per nine but gradually improved as his long career played out; for him to go from 6.2 walks per nine with the 1966 Greenville Mets to 3.7 with the 1989 Texas Rangers represents a 40 percent reduction. An equivalent improvement by Dalkowski would still have left him walking over 11 batters per nine innings.

Dalkowski was like *The Room* of pitchers, a player so bad he became good again. Cal Ripken, Sr., who both played with and managed Dalkowski, recalled in a 1979 *Sporting News* "where are they now" piece the occasion when the pitcher crossed up his catcher and his fastball, "hit the plate umpire smack in the mask. The mask broke all to pieces and the umpire wound up in the hospital for three days with a concussion. If they ever had a radar gun in those days, I'll bet Dalkowski would have been timed at 110 miles an hour."

Signed by the Orioles out of New Britain High in Connecticut in 1957, Dalkowski was sent to Kingsport in the Appalachian League, where he pitched 62 innings. He allowed only 22 hits in 62 innings, or 3.2 per nine, a number with no equivalent in major league history (though Aroldis Chapman came close in 2014), and also struck out 121 (17.6 per nine) and walked 129 (18.7). He was also charged with 39 wild pitches. That June, one of his fastballs clipped a Dodgers prospect named Bob Beavers and carried away part of his ear. "The first pitch was over the backstop, the second pitch was called a strike, I didn't think it was," Beavers said last year. "The third pitch hit me and knocked me out, so I don't remember much after that. I couldn't get in the sun for a while, and I never did play baseball again." Former minor leaguer Ron Shelton based the *Bull Durham* pitcher Nuke LaLoosh on Dalkowski. And yet, to see him as a figure of fun, an amusing loser, is to misunderstand something unique and strange.

Dalkowski kept on posting some of the strangest lines in baseball history. Pitching for the Stockton Ports of the Class C California League in 1960, he struck out 262 and walked 262 in 170 innings. Yet, he did improve, especially after pitching for Earl Weaver at Elmira in 1962. Weaver had previously had Dalkowski at Aberdeen in 1959, but wasn't ready to grapple with him then. This time he was. "I had grown more and more concerned about players with great physical abilities who could not learn to correct certain basic deficiencies no matter how much you instructed or drilled them," he related in his autobiography, *It's What You Learn After You Know It All That Counts*. He got permission from the Orioles to give all of his players the Stanford-Binet IQ test. "Dalkowski finished in the 1 percentile in his ability to understand facts. Steve, it was said to say, had the ability to do everything but learn." [sic]

IQ tests are problematic diagnostic tools, so take Weaver's estimate of Dalkowski's mental capabilities with a grain of salt. What's important is that even if he got to the right answer by way of the wrong reason, Weaver had learned something valuable. His insight was to stop asking Dalkowski to learn new pitches and just let him get by with the two that he had. Were Dalkowski a prospect today, that would have been a no-brainer: Can't develop a third pitch? The bullpen is right over there, sir. Player development wasn't like that then, but Weaver, temporarily Dalkowski's mentor, could let him work with what he had. According to Weaver, the pitcher responded: "In the final 57 innings he pitched that season Dalkowski gave up 1 earned run, struck out 110 batters, and walked only 11." It's not true—as per the *Elmira Star-Gazette*, as of late July, Dalkowski had walked 71 in 106 innings and finished with 114 in 160 innings, which means Dalkowski's control actually faded at the end of the season rather than improved—but that doesn't mean it didn't happen in some sense, just that it didn't happen that way. Again, it's the journey, not the destination, and his ERA was 3.04 so *something* had gone right.

Also along the way: The next spring, Orioles manager Billy Hitchcock was rooting for Dalkowski to make the team as a long-man—maybe Weaver had gotten through to him. There were things out of Weaver's control, like the universe's twisted sense of humor: that March, Dalkowski's elbow went "twang."

You sometimes read that it was the Orioles' insistence on Dalkowski learning the curve that did him in, but even if they hadn't learned their lesson, the injury was probably just a coincidence: Dalkowski had thrown an incredible number of pitches over the previous few years. Still, it testifies to the dangers of trying to get what you want and risking the loss of what you had. Dalkowski tried to come back, but the 110-mph stuff was gone. A pitcher with no control and no stuff is…a civilian. What followed were years of vagabond living, arrests for drunkenness. There were Alcoholics Anonymous meetings, assistance from baseball alumni associations, but none of it took. From the 1990s until the time of his passing he dwelt in an assisted living facility, suffering from alcohol-related dementia. He'd been a heavy drinker since his teenage years. As with all those pitches per game, there was a price to be paid. You make choices on the journey and some of them are irrevocable. It's like a fairy tale: "Bite of poison apple? Don't mind if I do."

In the aforementioned *Sporting News* profile, Chuck Stevens, the head of the Association of Professional Ballplayers of America, a ballplayer charity, said, "I've got nothing against drinking. I do it myself sometimes. But, I don't condone common drunkenness. We went through lots of heartache and many dollars, but Dalkowski didn't want to help himself and we weren't going to keep him drunk." The journey is *un*like a fairy tale: No one will come along and kiss it better, not if they're busy forming judgments.

In the end, we are left with a sort of philosophical chicken/egg conundrum: Is failing to meet your goals evidence of unfulfilled potential or the lack of it? Isn't what you did by definition what you were capable of doing? Or could you have broken through to something better with the right help, the right lucky break? These are unanswerable questions, and how we try to answer them may say more about us than about the people we're judging.

No pitcher ever has it easy. *All* pitchers must work hard. *All* pitchers must refine their craft. It's almost never just about *stuff*. Dalkowski dreaming is no insult to the great pitchers who made it; from Pete Alexander to Max Scherzer, they have all earned their way up. And yet, if it is true that we can only do as much as we can do, then the journey would be more of an adventure, the ultimate triumph or defeat more noble, if like Dalkowski we lacked 100 percent of the confidence, the command, the self-possession, the commitment, the resistance to making bad decisions that so many great players possess—to be gloriously human. Or, to put it more succinctly, it would be fun to be able to throw as hard as any person ever has. Even if just for a moment, and even if nothing more came of it than that, no one could say you hadn't lived life to the fullest.

—*Steven Goldman is an author of Baseball Prospectus.*

A Reward For A Functioning Society

by Cory Frontin and Craig Goldstein

On July 5, Nationals reliever Sean Doolittle said in the middle of a press conference regarding the restart of Major League Baseball and what would later be known as summer camp, "sports are like the reward of a functioning society." This sentence was amidst a much longer, thoughtful reply about the societal and health conditions under which MLB players were being brought back. It's a very similar sentiment to one Jane McManus used on April 7, when she discussed the White House's meeting with sports commissioners. She said "sports are the effect of a functioning society—not the precursor."

Both versions of the same sentiment spoke to a laudable ideal in the context of a country that was not addressing a rampaging virus, and opting instead to bring sports back for the feeling of normalcy rather than the reality of it. "Priorities," as McManus said.

On Wednesday, the NBA's Milwaukee Bucks conducted a wildcat/political strike, refusing to come out for Game 5 of their playoff series against the Orlando Magic. The Magic refused to accept the forfeit, and shortly thereafter other playoff series were threatened by player strikes. Eventually the league moved to postpone that day's games, folding to players leveraging their united power.

The backdrop against which these actions took place was the shooting by police of Jacob Blake. Blake was shot in the back seven times by police, as he attempted to get into his vehicle. He managed to survive the assault, but is paralyzed from the waist down.

⚾ ⚾ ⚾

The step taken to walk out, first by the Milwaukee Bucks, then subsequently by other NBA, WNBA, and MLB teams, was a step toward upholding the virtue of the sentiment described by McManus and Doolittle. But that sentiment does not align with the broad history of sports in this and other countries, a history that contradicts the core of the idealistic statement.

Sports have been a significant part of American society for most of its existence, expanding in importance and influence in recent years. The idea that society was functioning in a way that was worthy of the reward of sports for most of that time is laughable. Much of America is not functioning and has not functioned for Black people, full stop. The oppressed people at the center of this political act by players, specifically Black players, in concert throughout the NBA and in fits and starts throughout Major League Baseball, have not known a society that functions for them rather than *because* of them.

Politics has been part of the sports landscape since the inception of sport, but for just about as long people have bemoaned its presence. Sports are to be an escape, it is said. An escape from what, though? A functioning society?

No, the presence of sports has never signified a cultural or political system that is on the up and up. Rather, the presence of sports *reflect and reinforce the society that produces them.*

⚾ ⚾ ⚾

The Negro Leagues were born out of societal dysfunction. The need for entirely separate leagues, composed of Black and Latino players barred from the Major Leagues because of racism? That is not a functioning society, and yet there were sports.

Even the integration of players from the Negro Leagues resulted in a transfer of power and wealth from Black-owned businesses and communities and into white ones, mirroring the dysfunction that had bled into every aspect of American society at the time. Japheth Knopp noted in the Spring 2016 Baseball Research Journal:

> *The manner in which integration in baseball—and in American businesses generally—occurred was not the only model which was possible. It was likely not even the best approach available, but rather served the needs of those in already privileged positions who were able to control not only the manner in which desegregation occurred, but the public perception of it as well in order to exploit the situation for financial gain. Indeed, the very word integration may not be the most applicable in this context because what actually transpired was not so much the fair and equitable combination of two subcultures into one equal and more homogenous group, but rather the reluctant allowance—under certain preconditions—for African Americans to be assimilated into white society.*

To understand the value of a movement, though, is not to understand how it is co-opted by ownership, but to know the people it brings together and what they demand. When Jackie Robinson—the player who demarcated the inevitability of the end of the Negro leagues—attended the March on Washington for Jobs and Freedom in 1963, he did so with his family and marched alongside the people. He stood alongside hundreds of thousands to fight for their common civil and labor rights. "The moral arc of the universe is long," many freedom fighters have echoed, "but it bends towards justice." The bend, it is less frequently said, happens when a great mass of people place the moral arc of the universe on their knee and apply force, as Jackie, his family, and thousands of others did that day.

⚾ ⚾ ⚾

Of course, taking the moral arc of the universe down from the mantle and bending it is not without risk. Perhaps the outsized influence of athletes is itself a mark of a dysfunctional society, but, nonetheless, hundreds of athletes woke up on Wednesday morning with the power to bring in millions of dollars in revenues. That very power, as we would come to find out, was matched with the equal and opposite power to *not* bring those revenues. That power, in hands ranging from the Milwaukee Bucks, to Kenny Smith in the *Inside the NBA* Studio, from the unexpected ally, Josh Hader, and his largely white teammates to the notably Black Seattle Mariners, would be exercised for a single demand: the end to state violence against Black people. Not unlike the March itself, it sat at the intersection of the civil rights of Black Americans and bold labor action. The March on Washington stood in the face of a false notion of integration—against an integration of extraction but not one of equality—and proposed something different. Just the same, the acts of solidarity of August 26, 2020 will be remembered in stark defiance of MLB's BLM-branded, but ultimately empty displays on opening weekend.

Bold defiance like this can never be without risk. By choosing to exercise this power, the Milwaukee Bucks took a risk. They risked vitriol and backlash from those they disagreed with. They risked fines or seeing their contracts voided, as a walkout like this is prohibited by their CBA. They risked forfeiting a playoff game, one that, as the No. 1 seed in the playoffs, they'd worked all year to attain. They didn't know how Orlando would respond. It wasn't clear that other teams throughout the league would follow suit in solidarity. And it wasn't known the league would accept these actions and moderately co-opt them by "postponing" games that would have featured no players.

If the league reschedules the games, some of the athletes' risk—their shared sacrifice—will be diminished, in retrospect. But they did not know any of that when they took that risk. And it is often left to athletes to take these risks when others in society won't, especially those of their same socioeconomic status and levels of influence.

It is athletes, specifically BIPOC athletes, that take them, though, because they live with the risk of being something other than white in this country every day. They are no strangers to the realities of police brutality. It seems incongruous then, to say that sports are a reward for a functioning society when we rely on athletes to lead us closer to being a functioning society. Luckily, our beloved athletes, WNBA players first and foremost among them, understand what sports truly are: a pipebender for the moral arc of the universe.

—Craig Goldstein is editor in chief of Baseball Prospectus. Cory Frontin is an author of Baseball Prospectus.

Index of Names

Alexander, Tyler	38	Grossman, Robbie	79
Baddoo, Akil	72	Hill, Derek	80
Bonifacio, Jorge	14	Jiménez, Joe	54
Boyd, Matthew	40	Jones, JaCoby	24
Brigham, Jake	84	Manning, Matt	87, 93
Burrows, Beau	85	Mazara, Nomar	26
Cabrera, Miguel	16	Meadows, Parker	81, 97
Cameron, Daz	73, 98	Mize, Casey	56, 92
Campos, Roberto	98	Norris, Daniel	58
Candelario, Jeimer	18	Núñez, Renato	28
Carpenter, Ryan	85	Paredes, Isaac	30, 95
Castro, Harold	74	Pérez, Franklin	88
Castro, Willi	20	Ramírez, Erasmo	60
Cisnero, José	42	Ramos, Wilson	32
Clemens, Kody	75	Reyes, Victor	34
Dingler, Dillon	75, 95	Rogers, Jake	82
Faedo, Alex	86, 96	Schoop, Jonathan	36
Farmer, Buck	44	Schreiber, John	62
Fulmer, Michael	46	Skubal, Tarik	64, 94
Funkhouser, Kyle	48	Soto, Gregory	66
Garcia, Bryan	50	Stewart, Christin	83
Garcia, Greg	76	Torkelson, Spencer	84, 91
García, Rony	52	Turnbull, Spencer	68
Garneau, Dustin	76	Ureña, José	70
Goodrum, Niko	22	Wentz, Joey	89, 96
Greene, Riley	78, 92	Workman, Gage	98
Greiner, Grayson	78	Zimmermann, Jordan	90

For the Joy of Keeping Score

THIRTY81 Project is an ongoing graphic design project focused on the ballparks of baseball. Since being established in 2013, scorecards have been a fundemantal part of the effort. Each two-page card is uniquely ballpark-centric — there are 30 variants — and designed with both beginning and veteran scorekeepers in mind. Evolving over the years with suggestions from fans, broadcasters, and official scorers, the sheets are freely available to everyone as printable letter-size PDFs at the project webshop: www.THIRTY81Project.com

Download, Print, Score, Repeat ...

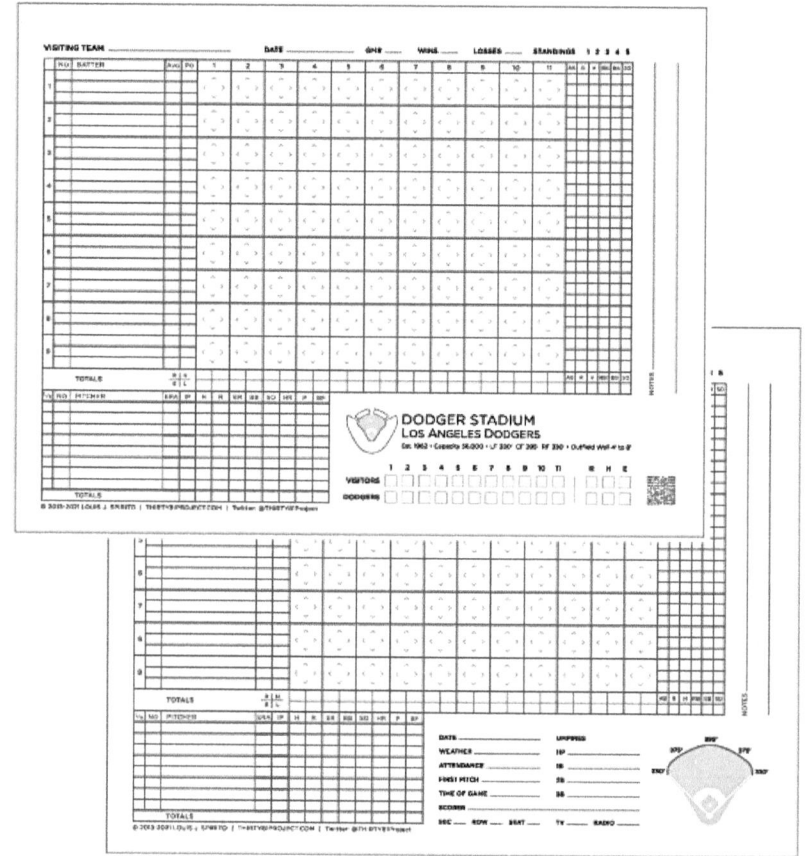

Scorecard design ©2013-2021 Louis J. Spirito | THIRTY81Project